The Complete Hamilton Beach Breakfast Sandwich Maker Cookbook

1200-Day Creative Breakfast Recipes to Enjoy Mouthwatering Sandwiches, Burgers, Omelets and More | For Beginners and Advanced Users.

Bordana Hefhalle

Table of Contents

Chapter 6: Normal Sandwiches and Omelets 66

Chapter 7: Vegetarian Sandwiches 76

Chapter 8: Snacks and Desserts Sandwich.. 97

INTRODUCTION

The Hamilton Beach Breakfast Sandwich Maker is a powerful cooker that, like a culinary artifact, brings us endless surprises and conveniences with its unique features. It prepared sandwiches within five minutes. The method of the cleaning process is simple. You can prepare different sandwiches using this kitchen appliance. You can use bread for making sandwiches and bagels, waffles, tortillas, pancakes, or biscuits.

The variety of ingredients in this book will satisfy your taste buds, whether it's savory meats, rich cheeses, or refreshing fruits and vegetables that can be combined to create a variety of rich and flavorful dishes.

Each of our recipes has been carefully compiled to provide you with the steps to prepare and cook them. Whether you are a beginner or a seasoned chef, you will be able to find the right recipe for your needs. With practice, every chef can master the basics of cooking independently.

Buy a copy of The Complete Hamilton Beach Breakfast Sandwich Maker Cookbook today so you can have a healthy morning meal in just 5 minutes.

Chapter 1: Hamilton Beach Breakfast Sandwich Maker

What is Hamilton Beach Breakfast Sandwich Maker?

The Hamilton Beach Breakfast Sandwich Maker is a satisfying kitchen appliance. You can prepare sandwiches within five minutes or less. The design of this appliance resembles the shape of English muffins. The assembly process of this appliance is easy. You can prepare a restaurant-style sandwich using a Hamilton Beach Breakfast Sandwich Maker.

The Hamilton Beach Breakfast Sandwich Maker comes with a cover/lid, cooking plate, bottom heating plate, indicator lights (green and red), cooking plate handle, removable ring assembly, top healthy plate, and base. Green light is used to preheat the sandwich maker. Red light is a power button, and it is used to turn off/on the sandwich maker.

When you are using this first time, open the cover/lid and remove the ring assembly. Rinse the removable ring assembly into the dishwasher or soapy and warm water. Then, dry it. Wipe the top and bottom heating plates with a soapy and damp cloth. Remove the soap with a damp cloth and dry it thoroughly.

Spray rings with non-stick cooking spray or brush with vegetable oil.

Benefits of Sandwich Maker

Breakfast Cooked Under 5 Minutes:

Everyone is busy in the morning. Moms want to prepare morning breakfast quickly for their families. Sometimes, they didn't prepare healthy breakfast for their families. Now, Hamilton Beach Breakfast Sandwich Maker makes your easier. You can prepare breakfast for your family in five minutes or less.

Easy to Clean:

All parts of the Hamilton Beach Breakfast Sandwich Maker are removable.

You can easily remove them from the sandwich maker and place them in the dishwasher. Wash with soapy water. Then, dry it. Return the parts to the sandwich maker.

Make Different Breakfast:

You can prepare a sandwich for the sandwich maker and prepare bagels, tortillas, biscuits, pancake sandwiches, savory sandwiches, meat or seafood sandwiches, sweet sandwiches, muffins, flatbread, croissants, and omelets.

One Dish Meal:

If you want to prepare a sandwich for your family in the morning, you need to assemble the ingredients like bread, tomato slices, eggs, and cheese, place them over the bread, and put them on the cooking plate. The Hamilton Beach Breakfast Sandwich Maker will prepare fried eggs, melted cheese, and toast bread.

Easy to Use:

The Hamilton Beach Breakfast Sandwich Maker is a user-friendly cooking appliance. You can prepare breakfast for your entire family in batches, and it will take less time. You didn't need to stand for 2 to 3 hours in the morning.

Steps for Using Sandwich Maker

1. Firstly, plug the cord into the outlet. The red button turns on the sandwich maker. The red button is used to turn on/off the sandwich maker.
2. Then, lightly spray the removable ring assembly with non-stick cooking spray.
3. The unit is preheated when the cover/lid is closed, and cooking plates are rotated into the rings.
4. The green light will be ON when the unit is preheated to an accurate temperature and will cycle ON/OFF during cooking.
5. It would be best if you used handles to lift over, cooking plates, and top ring.
6. Then, place half of the bread, a small bagel, a small biscuit, or a tortilla onto the bottom plate.
7. Then, top with remaining ingredients such as precooked cheese, seafood, meat, vegetables, or spices. But, don't overfill the breakfast sandwich maker. Then, lower the top ring and cooking plate.
8. Break an egg onto the cooking plate. Prick the egg with a fork. You can use egg whites, egg yolks, whole eggs, or scrambled eggs.
9. Then, place another half of bread, bagel, biscuit, or tortilla.
10. Close the cover or lid of the Hamilton Beach Breakfast Sandwich Maker for 4 to 5 minutes.
11. Wait for 2 minutes between cooking sandwiches to ensure the unit is heated to an accurate temperature.
12. When cooking time is completed, rotate the cooking plate handle.
13. Then, unplug the cooking appliance. Let them cool.

Tips and Tricks

1. Before using the breakfast sandwich maker, read all instructions.
2. Didn't allow the children to play with the appliance.
3. Prepare your ingredients before cooking sandwiches.
4. For best results, use buns, bagels, and bread to make sandwiches.
5. Always keep the lid closed with rings and a cooking plate in place when the unit is preheating.
6. Check the cooking plate before preheating when adding sandwich ingredients.
7. Wear the oven mitt and use handles to lift cooking plates.
8. Don't touch the hot surfaces of the breakfast sandwich maker.
9. Unplug from the wall outlet when not in use and before cleaning. Let them cool them.
10. Do not immerse the cooking unit into the water or any other liquid.
11. A breakfast sandwich maker is an indoor appliance. Do not use outdoors.
12. Don't put an appliance on the heating element or near the heating element.

13. Let them cool before cleaning them.

14. Don't remove the food with sharp utensils.

15. Adjust the cooking time on the breakfast sandwich maker.

16. Lower the lid without pressing it.

17. Press the red light to turn ON/OFF the breakfast sandwich maker.

18. Do not move the breakfast sandwich maker while in use.

19. If you have large-sized waffles or toast, cut them with a cookie-cutter.

20. When using meat, seafood, or vegetables, it should be pre-cooked and then placed into the sandwich maker.

21. Clean pantries, utensils, and work surfaces before using them.

22. Read the recipe two times before preparing breakfast.

23. Measure ingredients according to the recipe's instructions.

24. Taste the breakfast before serving.

25. Buy fresh veggies, meat, cheese, and eggs.

26. Don't overfill the cooking plate.

27. Don't use extra-large eggs; otherwise, they will leak from the unit.

28. Add more time for cooking if it is cooked well. This process is best for frozen ingredients. For best results, let thaw the ingredients at room temperature and then place them into the breakfast sandwich maker.

29. Adjust five minutes for cooking time.

Chapter 2: Eggs Sandwich

Egg Sandwich with Mayo Paste

Prep Time: 15 Minutes   Cook Time: 5 Minutes   Serves: 1

Preparation and Cooking Tips: you can also add a lettuce leaf to the filling.

Serving Suggestion: Would you please serve the sandwich with a broccoli salad on the side?

Ingredients:

- 2 slices bread, cut into 4 inches round
- 1 teaspoon crushed Calabrian chilies
- 2 teaspoons mayonnaise
- 1½ teaspoon olive oil
- 2 extra-large eggs
- 1 pinch kosher salt

Directions:

1. Preheat the Breakfast Sandwich Maker until the green PREHEAT light comes on.
2. Lift cover, top rings, and cooking plates.
3. Beat eggs with salt and oil in a bowl.
4. Place a bread slice inside the bottom tray of the sandwich maker. Spread mayonnaise on top of the bread.
5. Lower the cooking plate and top rings then pour in the egg.
6. Add chilies and the other bread slice on top.
7. Cover the top hood, and let the sandwich cook for 5 minutes.
8. Rotate the handle of the cooking plate clockwise until it stops.
9. Lift the hood, and the rings and transfer the sandwich to a plate.

Nutritional Value (Amount per Serving):

Calories: 376; Fat: 21g; Sodium: 476mg; Carbs: 2g; Fiber: 3g; Sugar: 4g; Protein: 20g

Beans Muffin and Egg Sandwich

Prep Time: 15 Minutes   Cook Time: 5 Minutes   Serves: 2

Preparation and Cooking Tips: You can also add a drizzle of paprika on top of the filling.

Serving Suggestion: Serve the sandwich with coleslaw and your favorite sauce on the side.

Ingredients:

- 1 ounce shredded Mexican cheese
- 1 tablespoon sliced green onion
- 2 tablespoons refried beans
- 2 English muffins
- 1 large egg

Directions:

1. Preheat the Breakfast Sandwich Maker until the green PREHEAT light comes on.
2. Lift cover, top rings, and cooking plates.
3. Place the lower half of the muffin in the sandwich maker then top it with ½ of the refried beans and cheese.
4. Lower the cooking plate and top rings, then pour in ½ of the egg.
5. Add green onion and the other half of the muffin on top.
6. Cover the top hood, and let the sandwich cook for 5 minutes.
7. When finished cooking, rotate the handle of the cooking plate clockwise until it stops.
8. Lift the hood, and the rings and transfer the sandwich to a plate.
9. Repeat the same steps with the remaining ingredients.

Nutritional Value (Amount per Serving):

Calories: 351; Fat: 16g; Sodium: 777mg; Carbs: 26g; Fiber: 4g; Sugar: 5g; Protein: 28g

Prosciutto Ham Sandwich

Prep Time: 15 Minutes   Cook Time: 7 Minutes   Serves: 2

Preparation and Cooking Tips: Add some additional dried herbs to the filling.

Serving Suggestion: Serve the sandwich with your favorite sauce on the side.

Ingredients:

- ¼ cup whey protein isolate
- 1 teaspoon xanthan gum
- ½ teaspoon baking powder
- ½ cup almond flour
- ½ cup egg whites
- 1 pepperoni slice
- 1 slice ham
- 1 slice prosciutto
- 1 cheese slices
- 1 slice tomatoes

Directions:

1. Mix almond flour with protein, gum, xanthan baking powder, and egg whites in a 4-inch ramekin.
2. Cook this bread batter in the microwave for 2 minutes then slice into 2 equal-sized slices.

3. Preheat the Breakfast Sandwich Maker until the green PREHEAT light comes on.
4. Lift cover, top rings, and cooking plates. Place the lower half of the bread in the sandwich maker.
5. Lower the cooking plate and top rings then place ½ of the fillings on top.
6. Add the other circle of the bread on top. Cover the top hood, and let the sandwich cook for 5 minutes.
7. When finished cooking, rotate the handle of the cooking plate clockwise until it stops.
8. Lift the hood, and the rings and transfer the sandwich to a plate.
9. Repeat the same steps with the remaining ingredients.

Nutritional Value (Amount per Serving):

Calories: 361; Fat: 16g; Sodium: 515mg; Carbs: 9.3g; Fiber: 0.1g; Sugar: 18.2g; Protein: 33.3g

Cauliflower and Avocado Bagel Sandwiches

Prep Time: 15 Minutes   Cook Time: 15 Minutes   Serves: 2

Preparation and Cooking Tips: Add a layer of spicy mayo and pickled veggies for a change of taste.

Serving Suggestion: Serve the sandwich with your favorite keto smoothie on the side.

Ingredients:

- 1 head cauliflower, cut into florets
- 1 teaspoon dried minced garlic
- 1 tablespoon dried minced onion
- 2 tablespoons almond flour
- 1 tablespoon coconut flour
- ½ teaspoon garlic powder
- ¼ teaspoon fine sea salt
- ½ teaspoon poppy seeds
- 1 tablespoon sesame seeds
- ½ teaspoon coarse sea salt
- 2 tablespoons mayonnaise
- ½ cup shredded cheddar
- 1 avocado, mashed
- 2 eggs

Directions:

1. At 350 degrees F, preheat your oven.
2. Blend cauliflower with almond flour, eggs, garlic powder, sea salt, coconut flour, poppy seeds, garlic and onion in a food processor.

3. Line a suitable baking sheet with parchment paper and divide the cauliflower mixture into 4-inch equal rounds with a hole at the center onto the baking sheet and drizzle seeds on top. Bake the cauliflower circles for 10 minutes until golden brown.
4. Preheat the Breakfast Sandwich Maker until the green PREHEAT light comes on. Lift cover, top rings, and cooking plates.
5. Split the baked bagels in half. Place one-half of a bagel in the sandwich maker.
6. Lower the cooking plate and top rings, then add ½ of cheddar, mayo, and avocado.
7. Place the other half of the bagel on top. Cover the top hood, and let the sandwich cook for 5 minutes.
8. Rotate the handle of the cooking plate clockwise until it stops. Lift the hood, and the rings and transfer the sandwich to a plate.
9. Repeat the same steps with the remaining ingredients.

Nutritional Value (Amount per Serving):

Calories: 245; Fat: 14g; Sodium: 122mg; Carbs: 8g; Fiber: 1.2g; Sugar: 12g; Protein: 4.3g

Spinach, Ham and Eggs Sandwich

Prep Time: 15 Minutes   Cook Time: 5 Minutes   Serves: 1

Preparation and Cooking Tips: You can also add lettuce leaves to the filling.

Serving Suggestion: Would you please serve the sandwich with crispy bacon and your favorite sauce on the side?

Ingredients:

- ½ cup baby spinach, washed and chopped
- 1 slice Cheddar cheese
- 1 teaspoon olive oil
- 1 English muffin
- 1 slice ham
- 1 egg
- Fresh basil (optional)

Directions:

1. In a small sauté pan, heat olive oil. Add spinach and sauté until just softened. Remove from heat.
2. In a small bowl, blend spinach and egg with a fork.
3. Preheat the Breakfast Sandwich Maker until the green PREHEAT light comes on.
4. Lift cover, top rings, and cooking plates.
5. Place the lower half of the muffin in the sandwich maker and top it with cheese, and ham.

6. Lower the cooking plate and top rings then pour in the egg.
7. Add the other half of the muffin on top. Cover the top hood, and let the sandwich cook for 5 minutes.
8. When finished cooking, rotate the handle of the cooking plate clockwise until it stops.
9. Lift the hood, and the rings and transfer the sandwich to a plate.

Nutritional Value (Amount per Serving):

Calories: 502; Fat: 25g; Sodium: 230mg; Carbs: 1.5g; Fiber: 0.2g; Sugar: 0.4g; Protein: 64.1g

Cheese and Egg Buttermilk Biscuit Sandwich

Prep Time: 15 Minutes   Cook Time: 5 Minutes   Serves: 1

Preparation and Cooking Tips: Add some additional dried herbs to the filling.

Serving Suggestion: Would you please serve the sandwich with crispy bacon and your favorite sauce on the side?

Ingredients:

- 1 slice of sharp cheddar cheese
- 1 buttermilk biscuit, cut in half
- 1 egg   • Milk   • Salt and black pepper

Directions:

1. In a bowl, crack the egg and add a bit of milk. Add a dash of salt and black pepper for flavor.
2. Use a whisk to whisk the egg and milk together.
3. Preheat the Breakfast Sandwich Maker until the green PREHEAT light comes on.
4. Lift cover, top rings, and cooking plates.
5. Place the lower half of the biscuit in the sandwich maker, then add cheese.
6. Now lower the cooking plate and top rings, then pour in the egg.
7. Add the other half of the biscuit on top. Cover the top hood, and let the sandwich cook for 5 minutes.
8. When finished cooking, rotate the handle of the cooking plate clockwise until it stops.
9. Lift the hood, and the rings and transfer the sandwich to a plate.

Nutritional Value (Amount per Serving):

Calories: 268; Fat: 10.4g; Sodium: 411mg; Carbs: 0.4g; Fiber: 0.1g; Sugar: 0.1g; Protein: 40.6g

Avocado and Fried Egg Sandwich

Prep Time: 15 Minutes   Cook Time: 5 Minutes   Serves: 4

Preparation and Cooking Tips: Add a layer of pickled veggies for a change of taste.

Serving Suggestion: Would you please serve the sandwich with crispy carrot chips on the side?

Ingredients:

Sandwich:
- 8 slices Italian bread, cut into 4 inches round
- 4 (¾-ounce) slices of provolone cheese
- 4 tablespoons butter, softened
- 8 slices ripe tomato
- 4 large eggs

Avocado mixture:
- 2 tablespoons chopped red onion
- ½ cup avocado, pitted, peeled
- ¼ teaspoon salt
- ⅛ teaspoon pepper

Directions:

1. Beat eggs with butter in a suitable bowl and keep it aside.
2. Mash avocado in a bowl then add red onion, black pepper, and salt and mix well.
3. Preheat the Breakfast Sandwich Maker until the green PREHEAT light comes on.
4. Lift cover, top rings, and cooking plates.
5. Place one bread slice inside the bottom tray of the sandwich maker. Spread ¼ of the avocado mixture on top.
6. Lower the cooking plate and top rings then pour in ¼ egg.
7. Place a tomato and cheese slice and the other half of the muffin on top. Cover the top hood, and let the sandwich cook for 5 minutes.
8. Rotate the handle of the cooking plate clockwise until it stops. Lift the hood, and the rings and transfer the sandwich to a plate.
9. Repeat the same steps with the remaining ingredients.

Nutritional Value (Amount per Serving):

Calories: 440; Fat: 14g; Sodium: 220mg; Carbs: 2g; Fiber: 0.2g; Sugar: 1g; Protein: 37g

Classic Caprese Sandwich

Prep Time: 15 Minutes   Cook Time: 5 Minutes   Serves: 2

Preparation and Cooking Tips: You can also add a drizzle of lemon juice on top of the filling.

Serving Suggestion: Serve the sandwich with crispy bacon and your favorite sauce on the side.

Ingredients:

- ¼ cup whey protein isolate
- 1 teaspoon xanthan gum
- ½ teaspoon baking powder
- 1 mozzarella cheese slice
- ½ cup almond flour
- 1 pepperoni slice
- ½ cup egg whites
- 1 slice tomatoes

Directions:

1. Mix almond flour with xanthan gum, protein, baking powder, and egg whites in a 4-inch ramekin.
2. Cook this bread batter in the microwave for 2 minutes the slice into 2 equal-sized slices.
3. Preheat the Breakfast Sandwich Maker until the green PREHEAT light comes on.
4. Lift cover, top rings, and cooking plates. Place the lower half of the bread in the sandwich maker.
5. Lower the cooking plate and top rings, then place ½ of the fillings on top.
6. Add the other circle of the bread on top. Cover the top hood, and let the sandwich cook for 5 minutes.
7. When finished cooking, rotate the handle of the cooking plate clockwise until it stops.
8. Lift the hood, and the rings and transfer the sandwich to a plate.
9. Repeat the same steps with the remaining ingredients.

Nutritional Value (Amount per Serving):

Calories: 354; Fat: 7.9g; Sodium: 704mg; Carbs: 6g; Fiber: 3.6g; Sugar: 6g; Protein: 18g

Herbed Pork and Cauliflower Sandwich

Prep Time: 15 Minutes   Cook Time: 5 Minutes   Serves: 6

Preparation and Cooking Tips: You can also add lettuce leaves to the filling.

Serving Suggestion: Serve the sandwich with coleslaw and your favorite sauce on the side.

Ingredients:

- 1 head riced cauliflower cooked
- 1½ cups cheddar cheese grated
- Dash teaspoon of ground mustard seed
- Dash teaspoon dried thyme
- 12 mozzarella Cheese, slices
- ⅛ teaspoon dried sage
- ⅛ teaspoon dried oregano
- Ground black pepper
- 1 cup pulled barbecue pork
- Butter for greasing
- Fresh parsley for garnishing
- 1 egg beaten

Directions:

1. At 350 degrees F, preheat your oven.
2. Blend cauliflower with egg, dried herbs, spices, and grated cheese in a blender until smooth.
3. Line a suitable baking sheet with parchment paper and divide the cauliflower mixture into 3-4-inch equal rounds onto the baking sheet. Bake the cauliflower circles for 5 minutes per side.
4. Preheat the Breakfast Sandwich Maker until the green PREHEAT light comes on. Lift cover, top rings, and cooking plates.
5. Place one circle of the cauliflower bread in the sandwich maker and top it with pork.
6. Top it with 1 mozzarella cheese slice. Now lower the cooking plate and top rings.
7. Add the other circle of the bread on top and brush it with butter. Cover the top hood, and let the sandwich cook for 5 minutes.
8. When finished cooking, rotate the handle of the cooking plate clockwise until it stops.
9. Lift the hood, and the rings and transfer the sandwich to a plate. Repeat the same steps with the remaining ingredients. Garnish with parsley.

Nutritional Value (Amount per Serving):

Ca Calories: 195; Fat: 3g; Sodium: 355mg; Carbs: 7.7g; Fiber: 1g; Sugar: 25g; Protein: 1g

Sausage, Zucchini, and Cheese Sandwich

Prep Time: 15 Minutes   Cook Time: 9 Minutes   Serves: 1

Preparation and Cooking Tips: You can also add a drizzle of lemon juice on top of the filling.

Serving Suggestion: Serve the sandwich with your favorite sauce on the side.

Ingredients:

- ¼ teaspoon fresh Italian parsley, chopped
- 1 (1.2-ounces) cooked pork sausage patty
- 1 (0.5-ounces) slice of Cheddar cheese
- ¼ cup grated zucchini
- 2 large egg
- Salt and black pepper

Directions:

1. Beat egg with zucchini, black pepper, salt, and parsley in a small bowl.
2. Set a pan with two 4-inch metal rings in it. Pour half of the prepared egg mixture into each ring and cook for 2 minutes per side.
3. Preheat the Breakfast Sandwich Maker until the green PREHEAT light comes on.
4. Lift cover, top rings, and cooking plates.
5. Place one-half of the egg in the sandwich maker.
6. Lower the cooking plate and top rings then add sausage patty and cheddar cheese.
7. Place the other top half of the egg circle on top. Cover the top hood, and let the sandwich cook for 5 minutes.
8. When finished cooking, rotate the handle of the cooking plate clockwise until it stops.
9. Lift the hood, and the rings and transfer the sandwich to a plate.

Nutritional Value (Amount per Serving):

Calories: 198; Fat: 14g; Sodium: 272mg; Carbs: 7g; Fiber: 1g; Sugar: 9.3g; Protein: 1.3g

Green Peas and Egg Sandwiches

Prep Time: 15 Minutes   Cook Time: 5 Minutes   Serves: 2

Preparation and Cooking Tips: Add a layer of pickled onions for a change of taste.

Serving Suggestion: Would you please serve the sandwich with a broccoli salad on the side?

Ingredients:

- 1½ ounces Parmigiano-Reggiano cheese, grated
- 4 slices multigrain bread, cut into 4 inches round
- 2 cups chopped mustard greens
- 6 ounces frozen green peas, thawed
- 2 tablespoons apple cider vinegar
- ¼ cup toasted walnut oil

- ¾ teaspoon black pepper • 4 large eggs, beaten
- 1 tablespoon olive oil   • ¼ teaspoon salt

Directions:

1. Blend greens, apple cider vinegar, black pepper, oil, salt, and peas in a food processor until smooth.
2. Preheat the Breakfast Sandwich Maker until the green PREHEAT light comes on.
3. Lift cover, top rings, and cooking plates.
4. Place a bread slice inside the bottom tray of the sandwich maker. Spread ½ of the oil, and pesto on top.
5. Now lower the cooking plate and top rings, then pour in ½ of the egg and add the cheese. Place another bread slice on top.
6. Cover the top hood, and let the sandwich cook for 5 minutes.
7. Rotate the handle of the cooking plate clockwise until it stops.
8. Lift the hood, and the rings and transfer the sandwich to a plate.
9. Repeat the same steps with the remaining ingredients.

Nutritional Value (Amount per Serving):

Calories: 301; Fat: 16g; Sodium: 412mg; Carbs: 3g; Fiber: 0.2g; Sugar: 1g; Protein: 28.2g

Egg-Prosciutto Muffin Sandwich

Prep Time: 15 Minutes   Cook Time: 5 Minutes   Serves: 1

Preparation and Cooking Tips: You can also add a drizzle of lemon juice on top of the filling.

Serving Suggestion: Serve the sandwich with your favorite sauce on the side.

Ingredients:

- 2 tablespoons Greek yogurt, unflavored
- 1 teaspoon half-and-half or milk
- 3 slices prosciutto, sliced
- 3 asparagus stalks, broiled
- 1 teaspoon Dijon mustard
- ⅛ teaspoons lemon juice
- 1 teaspoon olive oil
- 1 English muffin   • Chives, snipped
- Sea salt   • 1 egg

Directions:

1. In a small cup, combine yogurt, mustard and lemon juice. Set aside.
2. Preheat the Breakfast Sandwich Maker until the green PREHEAT light comes on.
3. Lift cover, top rings, and cooking plates.
4. Place the lower half of the muffin in the sandwich maker, then add asparagus and prosciutto.
5. Now lower the cooking plate and top rings, then pour in the egg.
6. Top with chives. Drizzle the yogurt mixture over top egg. Add the other top half of the muffin on top.
7. Cover the top hood, and let the sandwich cook for 5 minutes.
8. When finished cooking, rotate the handle of the cooking plate clockwise until it stops.
9. Lift the hood, and the rings and transfer the sandwich to a plate.

Nutritional Value (Amount per Serving):

Calories: 346; Fat: 16.1g; Sodium: 882mg; Carbs: 1.3g; Fiber: 0.5g; Sugar: 0.5g; Protein: 48.2g

BLT Sandwich with Yogurt

Prep Time: 15 Minutes   Cook Time: 5 Minutes   Serves: 1

Preparation and Cooking Tips: Add some additional ground black pepper to the filling.

Serving Suggestion: Serve the sandwich with your favorite sauce on the side.

Ingredients:

- 1 pita bread, cut in half, cut in 4-inch circle
- 3 bacon slices, cooked
- 2 leaves romaine lettuce
- 2 tablespoons yogurt
- 1 slice tomato   • 1 egg

Directions:

1. Preheat the Breakfast Sandwich Maker until the green PREHEAT light comes on.
2. Lift cover, top rings, and cooking plates.
3. Place one-half of the pita bread in the sandwich maker, then add lettuce, yogurt, bacon slices, and tomato.
4. Lower the cooking plate and top rings then pour in the egg.
5. Add the other half of the bread on top.
6. Cover the top hood, and let the sandwich cook for 5 minutes.

7. When finished cooking, rotate the handle of the cooking plate clockwise until it stops.
8. Lift the hood, and the rings and transfer the sandwich to a plate.

Nutritional Value (Amount per Serving):

Calories: 353; Fat: 5g; Sodium: 818mg; Carbs: 53.2g; Fiber: 4.4g; Sugar: 8g; Protein: 17.3g

Chicken Avocado Sandwich

Prep Time: 15 Minutes   Cook Time: 5 Minutes   Serves: 2

Preparation and Cooking Tips: Add some additional dried herbs to the filling.

Serving Suggestion: Serve the sandwich with crispy bacon and your favorite sauce on the side.

Ingredients:

- 4 ounces grilled chicken breast
- ¼ cup whey protein isolate
- 1 teaspoon xanthan gum
- ½ teaspoon baking powder
- ½ cup almond flour   • 3 slices of tomato
- ½ cup egg whites   • 2 slices cheese
- ½ avocado mashed   • Salt and black pepper

Directions:

1. Mix almond flour with protein, xanthan gum, baking powder, and egg whites in a 4-inch ramekin.
2. Cook this bread batter in the microwave for 2 minutes the slice into 2 equal-sized slices.
3. Preheat the Breakfast Sandwich Maker until the green PREHEAT light comes on.
4. Lift cover, top rings, and cooking plates. Place the lower half of the bread in the sandwich maker.
5. Lower the cooking plate and top rings then place ½ of the fillings on top.
6. Add the other circle of the bread on top. Cover the top hood, and let the sandwich cook for 5 minutes.
7. When finished cooking, rotate the handle of the cooking plate clockwise until it stops.
8. Lift the hood, and the rings and transfer the sandwich to a plate.
9. Repeat the same steps with the remaining ingredients.

Nutritional Value (Amount per Serving):

Calories: 361; Fat: 10g; Sodium: 218mg; Carbs: 6g; Fiber: 10g; Sugar: 30g; Protein: 14g

Cuban Bacon and Tomato Sandwich

Prep Time: 15 Minutes   Cook Time: 5 Minutes   Serves: 2

Preparation and Cooking Tips: Add some additional ground black pepper to the filling.

Serving Suggestion: Serve the sandwich with crispy bacon and your favorite sauce on the side.

Ingredients:

- ¼ cup whey protein isolate
- 1 teaspoon xanthan gum
- ½ teaspoon baking powder
- ½ cup almond flour
- ½ cup egg whites
- 1 pepperoni slice
- 1 slice bacon
- ¼ cup pulled pork
- 1 cheese slices
- 1 slice tomatoes

Directions:

1. Mix almond flour with xanthan gum, protein, baking powder, and egg whites in a 4-inch ramekin.
2. Cook this bread batter in the microwave for 2 minutes the slice into 2 equal-sized slices.
3. Preheat the Breakfast Sandwich Maker until the green PREHEAT light comes on.
4. Lift cover, top rings, and cooking plates. Place the lower half of the bread in the sandwich maker.
5. Lower the cooking plate and top rings then place ½ of the fillings on top.
6. Add the other circle of the bread on top. Cover the top hood, and let the sandwich cook for 5 minutes.
7. When finished cooking, rotate the handle of the cooking plate clockwise until it stops.
8. Lift the hood, and the rings and transfer the sandwich to a plate.
9. Repeat the same steps with the remaining ingredients.

Nutritional Value (Amount per Serving):

Calories: 405; Fat: 22.7g; Sodium: 227mg; Carbs: 6.1g; Fiber: 1.4g; Sugar: 0.9g; Protein: 45.2g

Egg and Ham Sandwich with Hummus

Prep Time: 15 Minutes   Cook Time: 5 Minutes   Serves: 4

Preparation and Cooking Tips: Add a layer of spicy mayo and pickled veggies for a change of taste.

Serving Suggestion: Serve the sandwich with a cauliflower bacon salad on the side.

Ingredients:

Hummus:
- 2 cups chickpeas, cooked
- 1 garlic clove, crushed
- 1 lemon, juiced
- 1 tablespoon cumin
- ½ teaspoon salt
- ¼ cup olive oil
- ½ cup tahini

Sandwich:
- 8 bread slices, cut into 4 inches round
- 4 tomatoes, seeded and diced
- 2 cups ham, smoked and diced
- Oil, of choice, for brushing
- 2 garlic cloves, chopped
- 6 leaves basil, shredded
- 8 eggs, beaten
- ¼ cup olive oil
- 1 cup hummus
- Salt and black pepper

Directions:

1. Blend chickpeas with tahini, garlic, lemon juice, oil, salt, and cumin in a food processor.
2. Preheat the Breakfast Sandwich Maker until the green PREHEAT light comes on.
3. Lift cover, top rings, and cooking plates.
4. Place a bread slice inside the bottom tray of the sandwich maker. Top the bread with ¼ hummus and spread it evenly.
5. Beat the eggs with a tomato slice, sham, garlic, black pepper, salt, olive oil, and basil in a suitable bowl.
6. Lower the cooking plate and top rings, then pour in ¼ of the egg. Place another bread slice on top.
7. Cover the top hood, and let the sandwich cook for 5 minutes.
8. Rotate the handle of the cooking plate clockwise until it stops. Lift the hood, and the rings and transfer the sandwich to a plate.
9. Repeat the same steps with the remaining ingredients.

Nutritional Value (Amount per Serving):

Calories: 431; Fat: 20.1g; Sodium: 364mg; Carbs: 3g; Fiber: 1g; Sugar: 1.4g; Protein: 15g

Japanese Egg Sandwich

Prep Time: 15 Minutes   Cook Time: 5 Minutes   Serves: 1

Preparation and Cooking Tips: you can also add a lettuce

leaf to the filling.

Serving Suggestion: Serve the sandwich with crispy zucchini fries on the side.

Ingredients:

- 2 sandwich bread slices, cut into 4 inches round
- 1½ tablespoon Japanese mayonnaise
- 3 medium-boiled eggs peeled, mash
- ¼ teaspoon Dijon mustard
- ⅛ teaspoon white pepper
- ⅛ teaspoon onion powder
- 1 pinch salt

Directions:

1. Mix mayonnaise, white pepper, mustard, onion powder, and salt in a bowl. Stir in mashed eggs, then mix well.
2. Preheat the Breakfast Sandwich Maker until the green PREHEAT light comes on.
3. Lift cover, top rings, and cooking plates.
4. Place a bread slice inside the bottom tray of the sandwich maker.
5. Spread the egg mixture on top of the bread.
6. Now lower the cooking plate and top rings. Place a bread slice on top.
7. Cover the top hood, and let the sandwich cook for 5 minutes.
8. Rotate the handle of the cooking plate clockwise until it stops.
9. Lift the hood, and the rings and transfer the sandwich to a plate.

Nutritional Value (Amount per Serving):

Calories: 352; Fat: 2.4g; Sodium: 216mg; Carbs: 6g; Fiber: 2.3g; Sugar: 1.2g; Protein: 27g

Egg and Chorizo Torta with Avocado

Prep Time: 15 Minutes   Cook Time: 5 Minutes   Serves: 4

Preparation and Cooking Tips: You can also add lettuce leaves to the filling.

Serving Suggestion: Serve the sandwich with your favorite sauce on the side.

Ingredients:

- 1 tablespoon feta cheese or queso fresco, crumbled
- 1 round flatbread, sliced, cut into a 4-inch circle
- ½ avocado, cleaned, pitted and sliced
- 2 ounces Monterey jack, shredded
- 1 chorizo sausage patty, cooked
- 1 large egg

Directions:

1. Preheat the Breakfast Sandwich Maker until the green PREHEAT light comes on.
2. Lift cover, top rings, and cooking plates.
3. Place one bread slice in the sandwich maker then add cheese on top.
4. Now lower the cooking plate and top rings then add ¼ th of the rest of the fillings.
5. Place another bread slice on top.
6. Cover the top hood, and let the sandwich cook for 5 minutes.
7. When finished cooking, rotate the handle of the cooking plate clockwise until it stops.
8. Lift the hood, and the rings and transfer the sandwich to a plate.
9. Repeat the same steps with the remaining ingredients.

Nutritional Value (Amount per Serving):

Calories: 374; Fat: 13g; Sodium: 552mg; Carbs: 25g; Fiber: 1.2g; Sugar: 1.2g; Protein: 37.7g

Anchovy and Egg Sandwich

Prep Time: 15 Minutes   Cook Time: 15 Minutes   Serves: 4

Preparation and Cooking Tips: Add a layer of pickled veggies for a change of taste.

Serving Suggestion: Serve the sandwich with crispy bacon and your favorite sauce on the side.

Ingredients:

- 10 ounces canned or boxed tomato purée
- 1½ teaspoon fresh ground fennel seeds
- 1½ teaspoon ground coriander
- 8 slices sharp cheddar cheese
- 4 hamburger buns, split in half
- 1 tablespoon light brown sugar
- 2 tablespoons lemon juice
- 1 teaspoon dried oregano
- 1 large shallot, diced
- 1 garlic clove, minced
- 1 anchovy fillet
- 1 teaspoon salt
- black pepper, to taste
- 8 eggs, beaten
- 8 slices bacon, cooked

Directions:

1. Sauté shallot and garlic with oil in a skillet for 3

minutes.

2. Stir in coriander, fennel seeds, brown sugar, anchovy fillet, lemon juice, tomato puree, oregano, black pepper, and salt. Mix well and cook for 7 minutes on low heat with occasional stirring.

3. Beat eggs with black pepper and salt in a bowl.

4. Preheat the Breakfast Sandwich Maker until the green PREHEAT light comes on. Lift cover, top rings, and cooking plates.

5. Place one bread slice inside the bottom tray of the sandwich maker. Top it with ¼ of the tomato jam.

6. Lower the cooking plate and top rings then pour in ¼ of the egg mixture.

7. Add a slice of cheddar cheese, bacon slice, and another bread slice on top. Cover the top hood, and let the sandwich cook for 5 minutes.

8. Rotate the handle of the cooking plate clockwise until it stops. Lift the hood, and the rings and transfer the sandwich to a plate.

9. Repeat the same steps with the remaining ingredients.

Nutritional Value (Amount per Serving):

Calories: 405; Fat: 20g; Sodium: 941mg; Carbs: 6.1g; Fiber: 0.9g; Sugar: 0.9g; Protein: 45.2g

Beef and Cheddar Sandwich

Prep Time: 15 Minutes   Cook Time: 9 Minutes   Serves: 1

Preparation and Cooking Tips: Add some additional ground black pepper to the filling.

Serving Suggestion: Serve the sandwich with crispy bacon and your favorite sauce on the side.

Ingredients:

- ¼ teaspoon fresh Italian parsley, chopped
- ¼ teaspoon fresh basil, chopped
- 1 beef steak, cooked and sliced
- 1 tablespoon pesto
- 1 cheddar slice
- 1 tomato slice
- 2 large egg
- Salt and black pepper

Directions:

1. Beat egg with basil, black pepper, salt, and parsley in a small bowl.

2. Set a pan with two 4-inch metal rings in it.

3. Pour half of the prepared egg mixture into each ring and cook for 2 minutes per side.

4. Preheat the Breakfast Sandwich Maker until the green PREHEAT light comes on.

5. Lift cover, top rings, and cooking plates. Place one-half of the egg in the sandwich maker.

6. Lower the cooking plate and top rings then add beef, pesto, cheese, and tomato slices.

7. Place the other top half of the egg circle on top. Cover the top hood, and let the sandwich cook for 5 minutes.

8. When finished cooking, rotate the handle of the cooking plate clockwise until it stops.

9. Lift the hood, and the rings and transfer the sandwich to a plate.

Nutritional Value (Amount per Serving):

Calories: 153; Fat: 1g; Sodium: 8mg; Carbs: 6.6g; Fiber: 0.8g; Sugar: 56g; Protein: 1g

Celery and Egg Salad Sandwich

Prep Time: 15 Minutes   Cook Time: 5 Minutes   Serves: 1

Preparation and Cooking Tips: Add a layer of spicy mayo and pickled veggies for a change of taste.

Serving Suggestion: Serve the sandwich with crispy bacon and your favorite sauce on the side.

Ingredients:

- 1 hard-boiled large egg, peeled and chopped
- 1 tablespoon chopped green onion or chives
- 2 white bread slices, cut into 4 inches round
- 2 tablespoons mayonnaise, to taste
- 2 tablespoons chopped celery
- 1 pinch of curry powder
- 1 Lettuce leaf
- Salt and black pepper

Directions:

1. Mix mayonnaise with green onion, curry powder, celery, black pepper, and salt in a bowl.

2. Preheat the Breakfast Sandwich Maker until the green PREHEAT light comes on.

3. Lift cover, top rings, and cooking plates.

4. Place a bread slice inside the bottom tray of the sandwich maker.

5. Spread the mayonnaise mixture, lettuce leaf, and chopped eggs on top.

6. Now lower the cooking plate and top rings. Place the other bread slice on top.

7. Cover the top hood, and let the sandwich cook for 5

minutes.

8. Rotate the handle of the cooking plate clockwise until it stops.
9. Lift the hood, and the rings and transfer the sandwich to a plate.

Nutritional Value (Amount per Serving):

Calories: 388; Fat: 8g; Sodium: 611mg; Carbs: 8g; Fiber: 0g; Sugar: 4g; Protein: 13g

Deli Ham and Poppy Seeds Sliders

Prep Time: 15 Minutes   Cook Time: 7 Minutes   Serves: 1

Preparation and Cooking Tips: Add some additional dried herbs to the filling.

Serving Suggestion: Serve the slider with your favorite keto sauce on the side.

Ingredients:

- 1 tablespoon minced white onion
- ¼ teaspoon Worcestershire sauce
- ¼ cup whey protein isolate
- ½ teaspoon baking powder
- 2 tablespoons unsalted butter
- ¼ tablespoon yellow mustard
- ¼ tablespoon poppy seeds
- 1 teaspoon xanthan gum
- ½ cup egg whites
- ¼ lb. uncured deli ham
- ¼ lb. Swiss cheese
- ½ cup almond flour

Directions:

1. Mix almond flour with xanthan gum, protein, baking powder, and egg whites in a 4-inch ramekin.
2. Cook this bread batter in the microwave for 2 minutes the slice into 2 equal-sized slices.
3. Mix Worcestershire sauce, mustard, mustard, and onion in a bowl.
4. Preheat the Breakfast Sandwich Maker until the green PREHEAT light comes on.
5. Lift cover, top rings, and cooking plates. Place a bread slice in the sandwich maker.
6. Lower the cooking plate and top rings then place all the fillings on top.
7. Add the other circle of the bread on top. Cover the top hood, and let the sandwich cook for 5 minutes.
8. Rotate the handle of the cooking plate clockwise until it stops.
9. Lift the hood, and the rings and transfer the

sandwich to a plate.

Nutritional Value (Amount per Serving):

Calories: 361; Fat: 16g; Sodium: 515mg; Carbs: 9.3g; Fiber: 0.1g; Sugar: 18.2g; Protein: 33.3g

Classic Muffuletta Sandwich

Prep Time: 15 Minutes   Cook Time: 5 Minutes   Serves: 1

Preparation and Cooking Tips: Add some additional dried herbs to the filling.

Serving Suggestion: Serve the sandwich with coleslaw and your favorite sauce on the side.

Ingredients:

- 1 tablespoon roasted red bell pepper, drained and chopped
- 1 tablespoon pimento-stuffed green olives, chopped
- 2 slices French bread, cut into 4-inch circles
- 1 slice provolone cheese
- 1 slice ham, cooked
- 1 egg

Directions:

1. Preheat the Breakfast Sandwich Maker until the green PREHEAT light comes on.
2. Lift cover, top rings, and cooking plates.
3. Place one of the bread slices in the sandwich maker, and put the ham, cheese, green olives, and red bell peppers on it.
4. Now lower the cooking plate and top rings, then pour in the egg.
5. Add the other circle of the bread on top.
6. Cover the top hood, and let the sandwich cook for 5 minutes.
7. When finished cooking, rotate the handle of the cooking plate clockwise until it stops.
8. Lift the hood, and the rings and transfer the sandwich to a plate.

Nutritional Value (Amount per Serving):

Calories: 456; Fat: 16.4g; Sodium: 1321mg; Carbs: 19.2g; Fiber: 2.2g; Sugar: 4.2g; Protein: 55.2g

Mayo Bacon Chaffle Sandwich

Prep Time: 15 Minutes   Cook Time: 10 Minutes   Serves: 1

Preparation and Cooking Tips: Add some additional veggies to the filling.

Serving Suggestion: Serve the sandwich with your favorite keto salad on the side.

Ingredients:

Sandwich:
- 1 bacon slice, cooked
- 1 tablespoon mayo
- 1 lettuce leaf
- 1 tomato slice

Chaffle bread:
- 1 tablespoon green onion diced
- ½ cup mozzarella shredded
- ½ teaspoon Italian seasoning
- 1 egg

Directions:

1. Mix mozzarella cheese, egg, green onion, and seasoning in a bowl.
2. Set a non-stick skillet over medium heat.
3. Drop ½ of the cheese mixture into the skillet, spread it into 4 inches round, and cook for 2 minutes per side.
4. Make another chaffle and keep them aside.
5. Preheat the Breakfast Sandwich Maker until the green PREHEAT light comes on.
6. Lift cover, top rings, and cooking plates. Place a chaffle in the sandwich maker.
7. Spread mayo, tomato, lettuce, and bacon on top. Add the other circle of the chaffle on top.
8. Now lower the cooking plate and top rings. Cover the top hood, and let the sandwich cook for 5 minutes.
9. Rotate the handle of the cooking plate clockwise until it stops. Lift the hood, and the rings and transfer the sandwich to a plate.

Nutritional Value (Amount per Serving):

Calories: 361; Fat: 16g; Sodium: 515mg; Carbs: 9.3g; Fiber: 0.1g; Sugar: 18.2g; Protein: 33.3g

Pepper, Egg, and Cheese Sandwich

Prep Time: 15 Minutes   Cook Time: 5 Minutes   Serves: 1

Preparation and Cooking Tips: Add some additional ground black pepper to the filling.

Serving Suggestion: Serve the sandwich with your favorite sauce on the side.

Ingredients:

- 2 slices multigrain bread, cut into 4-inch circle
- 2 slices fresh red pepper
- 1-ounce goat cheese
- 1 slice red onion
- 1 large egg, beaten
- Salt and black pepper

Directions:

1. Preheat the Breakfast Sandwich Maker until the green PREHEAT light comes on.
2. Lift cover, top rings, and cooking plates.
3. Place one bread slice in the sandwich maker.
4. Top the bread with goat cheese, red pepper, and red onion.
5. Season with salt and black pepper to taste.
6. Now lower the cooking plate and top rings, then pour in the egg.
7. Add the other circle of the bread on top. Cover the top hood, and let the sandwich cook for 5 minutes.
8. When finished cooking, rotate the handle of the cooking plate clockwise until it stops.
9. Lift the hood, and the rings and transfer the sandwich to a plate.

Nutritional Value (Amount per Serving):

Calories: 546; Fat: 33.1g; Sodium: 1201mg; Carbs: 30g; Fiber: 2.4g; Sugar: 9.7g; Protein: 32g

Cauliflower and Cheddar Sandwich

Prep Time: 15 Minutes   Cook Time: 5 Minutes   Serves: 6

Preparation and Cooking Tips: You can also add lettuce leaves to the filling.

Serving Suggestion: Serve the sandwich with coleslaw and your favorite sauce on the side.

Ingredients:

- 1 head riced cauliflower cooked
- 1½ cups cheddar cheese, grated
- Dash teaspoon of ground mustard seed
- 12 mozzarella Cheese, slices
- Fresh parsley for garnishing
- ⅛ teaspoon dried sage
- ⅛ teaspoon dried oregano
- Dash teaspoon dried thyme
- Ground black pepper
- Butter for greasing
- 1 egg, beaten

Directions:

1. At 350 degrees F, preheat your oven.

2. Blend cauliflower with dried thyme, egg, spices, and grated cheese in a blender until smooth.
3. Line a suitable baking sheet with parchment paper and divide the cauliflower mixture into 3-4-inch equal rounds onto the baking sheet. Bake the cauliflower circles for 5 minutes per side.
4. Preheat the Breakfast Sandwich Maker until the green PREHEAT light comes on. Lift cover, top rings, and cooking plates.
5. Place one circle of the cauliflower bread in the sandwich maker. Top it with 1 mozzarella cheese slice.
6. Now lower the cooking plate and top rings. Add the other circle of the bread on top and brush it with butter.
7. Cover the top hood, and let the sandwich cook for 5 minutes.
8. When finished cooking, rotate the handle of the cooking plate clockwise until it stops. Lift the hood, and the rings and transfer the sandwich to a plate.
9. Garnish with parsley. Repeat the same steps with the remaining ingredients.

Nutritional Value (Amount per Serving):

Calories: 301; Fat: 5g; Sodium: 340mg; Carbs: 4.7g; Fiber: 1.2g; Sugar: 1.3g; Protein: 15.3g

Bread-Cheese Pudding Sandwich

Prep Time: 15 Minutes   Cook Time: 7 Minutes   Serves: 1
Preparation and Cooking Tips: You can also add lettuce leaves to the filling.
Serving Suggestion: Serve the sandwich with crispy bacon and your favorite sauce on the side.

Ingredients:

- 2 tablespoons maple syrup or honey
- 1 chicken sausage patty, cooked
- 2 slices stale bread, cubed
- 2 tablespoons plain yogurt
- 1 tablespoon melted butter
- Pinch ground nutmeg   • 1 large egg, beaten
- 1 slice of Swiss cheese   • 1 large egg

Directions:

1. Arrange the chunks of bread in a small round ramekin. Whisk together the remaining ingredients and pour over the bread – do not stir.

2. Microwave the ramekin on high heat for 2 minutes until the pudding is firm and hot. Let cool for 5 minutes.
3. Preheat the Breakfast Sandwich Maker until the green PREHEAT light comes on.
4. Lift cover, top rings, and cooking plates. Place the half of the bread pudding in the sandwich maker.
5. Top the bread pudding with the sausage patty and a slice of Swiss cheese.
6. Now lower the cooking plate and top rings, then pour in the egg.
7. Add the other circle of the bread on top. Cover the top hood, and let the sandwich cook for 5 minutes.
8. When finished cooking, rotate the handle of the cooking plate clockwise until it stops.
9. Lift the hood, and the rings and transfer the sandwich to a plate.

Nutritional Value (Amount per Serving):

Calories: 379; Fat: 19g; Sodium: 184mg; Carbs: 12.3g; Fiber: 0.6g; Sugar: 2g; Protein: 37.7g

BLT Cauliflower Sandwich

Prep Time: 15 Minutes   Cook Time: 15 Minutes   Serves: 4
Preparation and Cooking Tips: You can also add a layer of your favorite keto sauce to the filling.
Serving Suggestion: Serve the sandwich with salad on the side.

Ingredients:

- 8 slices thick-cut bacon, cooked
- 1 small head cauliflower
- 3 tablespoons almond flour
- 1 tablespoon coconut flour
- ½ teaspoon garlic powder
- ½ teaspoon fine sea salt
- ¼ teaspoon baking powder
- 1 pinch of black pepper
- 2 teaspoons poppy seeds
- 1 large ripe tomato, sliced
- 4 leaves crispy leaf lettuce
- 4 tablespoons mayo
- 2 eggs

Directions:

1. At 350 degrees F, preheat your oven.
2. Blend cauliflower with almond flour, coconut flour, garlic powder, eggs, salt, baking powder, and black

pepper in a food processor.

3. Line a suitable baking sheet with parchment paper and divide the cauliflower mixture into 4-inch equal rounds onto the baking sheet and drizzle seeds on top. Bake the cauliflower circles for 5 minutes per side.

4. Preheat the Breakfast Sandwich Maker until the green PREHEAT light comes on.

5. Lift cover, top rings, and cooking plates. Place one circle of the cauliflower bread in the sandwich maker.

6. Spread 1 tablespoon mayo, 1 lettuce leaf, 1 tomato slice, and 2 bacon slices on top.

7. Now lower the cooking plate and top rings. Add the other circle of the cauliflower bread on top. Cover the top hood, and let the sandwich cook for 5 minutes.

8. Rotate the handle of the cooking plate clockwise until it stops. Lift the hood, and the rings and transfer the sandwich to a plate.

9. Repeat the same steps with the remaining ingredients.

Nutritional Value (Amount per Serving):

Calories: 217; Fat: 12g; Sodium: 79mg; Carbs: 8g; Fiber: 1.1g; Sugar: 18g; Protein: 5g

Parmesan Eggs Muffin with Marinara

Prep Time: 15 Minutes   Cook Time: 5 Minutes   Serves: 1

Preparation and Cooking Tips: You can also add a layer of your favorite sauce to the filling.

Serving Suggestion: Serve the sandwich with your favorite sauce on the side.

Ingredients:

- 1 English muffin (whole grain is best), split
- ⅛ cup of parmesan cheese
- ¼ cup of marinara sauce
- 1 large egg, beaten

Directions:

1. Preheat the Breakfast Sandwich Maker until the green PREHEAT light comes on.
2. Lift cover, top rings, and cooking plates.
3. Place the lower half of the muffin in the sandwich maker and top it with sauce.
4. Sprinkle the cup of parmesan cheese on top of the sauce.

5. Now lower the cooking plate and top rings, then pour in the egg.
6. Place another muffin half on top.
7. Cover the top hood, and let the sandwich cook for 5 minutes.
8. When finished cooking, rotate the handle of the cooking plate clockwise until it stops.
9. Lift the hood, and the rings and transfer the sandwich to a plate.

Nutritional Value (Amount per Serving):

Calories: 351; Fat: 11g; Sodium: 150mg; Carbs: 3.3g; Fiber: 0.2g; Sugar: 1g; Protein: 33.2g

Ham, Tofu, and Cheese Sandwich

Prep Time: 15 Minutes   Cook Time: 15 Minutes   Serves: 1

Preparation and Cooking Tips: Add some additional dried herbs to the filling.

Serving Suggestion: Serve the sandwich with your favorite sauce on the side.

Ingredients:

- ¼ cup whey protein isolate
- 1 teaspoon xanthan gum
- ½ teaspoon baking powder
- ½ cup almond flour   • 1 slice ham
- ½ cup egg whites   • 1 cheese slices
- 2 tofu slices

Directions:

1. Set a non-stick pan on medium heat and sear the tofu slices for 3 minutes per side.
2. Mix almond flour with xanthan gum, protein, baking powder, and egg whites in a 4-inch ramekin.
3. Cook this bread batter in the microwave for 2 minutes the slice into 2 equal-sized slices.
4. Preheat the Breakfast Sandwich Maker until the green PREHEAT light comes on.
5. Lift cover, top rings, and cooking plates. Place a bread slice in the sandwich maker.
6. Lower the cooking plate and top rings then place tofu, ham, and cheese on top.
7. Add the other circle of the bread on top. Cover the top hood, and let the sandwich cook for 5 minutes.
8. Rotate the handle of the cooking plate clockwise until it stops.
9. Lift the hood, and the rings and transfer the

sandwich to a plate.

Nutritional Value (Amount per Serving):

Calories: 361; Fat: 16g; Sodium: 515mg; Carbs: 9.3g; Fiber: 0.1g; Sugar: 18.2g; Protein: 33.3g

Boiled Egg Salad Muffin

Prep Time: 15 Minutes   Cook Time: 5 Minutes   Serves: 1

Preparation and Cooking Tips: Add some additional dried herbs to the filling.

Serving Suggestion: Serve the sandwich with coleslaw and your favorite sauce on the side.

Ingredients:

- 3 hard-boiled eggs, chopped roughly
- ⅓ cup of pepper jack cheese, shredded
- 2 whole grain English muffins, split
- 2 teaspoons of Dijon mustard
- ¼ cup of Greek yogurt
- 1 teaspoon of horseradish
- 2 teaspoons of honey
- Salt and black pepper

Directions:

1. In a bowl, combine the horseradish, honey, Dijon mustard, Greek yogurt, pepper, salt, and hard-boiled eggs. Stir together until well combined.
2. Preheat the Breakfast Sandwich Maker until the green PREHEAT light comes on.
3. Lift cover, top rings, and cooking plates. Place one bread slice in the sandwich maker.
4. Place about cheese on top of the English muffin bottom.
5. Then, spoon the egg salad mixture on top of the cheese.
6. Now lower the cooking plate and top rings. Place another muffin half on top.
7. Cover the top hood, and let the sandwich cook for 5 minutes.
8. When finished cooking, rotate the handle of the cooking plate clockwise until it stops. Lift the hood, and the rings and transfer the sandwich to a plate.
9. Repeat with the rest of the ingredients.

Nutritional Value (Amount per Serving):

Calories: 400; Fat: 32g; Sodium: 721mg; Carbs: 2.6g; Fiber: 0g; Sugar: 0g; Protein: 27.4g

Mayo Beef Sandwich

Prep Time: 15 Minutes   Cook Time: 17 Minutes   Serves: 1

Preparation and Cooking Tips: Add some additional black pepper to the filling.

Serving Suggestion: Serve the sandwich with your favorite keto dip on the side.

Ingredients:

- ¼ cup whey protein isolate
- 1 teaspoon xanthan gum
- ½ teaspoon baking powder
- 1 pinch ground black pepper
- 1 slice of sharp cheddar cheese
- 1 teaspoon mayonnaise
- ½ cup almond flour
- 1 pinch salt
- ½ tablespoon butter
- ¼ onion, sliced
- ½ cup egg whites
- 1 slice of rye bread
- ¼ lb. ground beef

Directions:

1. Mix almond flour with xanthan gum, protein, baking powder, and egg whites in a 4-inch ramekin. Cook this bread batter in the microwave for 2 minutes then slice into 2 equal-sized slices.
2. Mix beef with black pepper, salt, butter, and onion in a food processor for 1 minute. Make 1 patty out of this mixture. Sear the patty in a skillet for 5 minutes per side.
3. Preheat the Breakfast Sandwich Maker until the green PREHEAT light comes on.
4. Lift cover, top rings, and cooking plates.
5. Place one bread slice inside the bottom tray of the sandwich maker then spread 1 teaspoon mayonnaise on top.
6. Place a beef patty and a cheese slice on top of the mayo. Now lower the cooking plate and top rings.
7. Place another bread slice on top. Cover the top hood, and let the sandwich cook for 5 minutes.
8. Rotate the handle of the cooking plate clockwise until it stops.
9. Lift the hood, and the rings and transfer the sandwich to a plate.

Nutritional Value (Amount per Serving):

Calories: 361; Fat: 16g; Sodium: 515mg; Carbs: 9.3g; Fiber: 0.1g; Sugar: 18.2g; Protein: 33.3g

Watercress, Egg, and Beef Sandwich

Prep Time: 15 Minutes   Cook Time: 9 Minutes   Serves: 1

Preparation and Cooking Tips: Add some additional dried herbs to the filling.

Serving Suggestion: Would you please serve the sandwich with crispy bacon and your favorite sauce on the side?

Ingredients:

- ¼ teaspoon fresh Italian parsley, chopped
- 6 ounces freshly sliced rare roast beef
- ¼ teaspoon fresh basil, chopped
- ½ teaspoon grated lemon zest
- 1 cup watercress
- 2 large egg
- Salt and black pepper

Directions:

1. Beat egg with basil, black pepper, salt, and parsley in a small bowl.
2. Set a pan with two 4-inch metal rings in it.
3. Pour half of the prepared egg mixture into each ring and cook for 2 minutes per side.
4. Preheat the Breakfast Sandwich Maker until the green PREHEAT light comes on.
5. Lift cover, top rings, and cooking plates. Place one-half of the egg in the sandwich maker.
6. Lower the cooking plate and top rings then add the remaining fillings.
7. Place the other top half of the egg circle on top. Cover the top hood, and let the sandwich cook for 5 minutes.
8. When finished cooking, rotate the handle of the cooking plate clockwise until it stops.
9. Lift the hood, and the rings and transfer the sandwich to a plate.

Nutritional Value (Amount per Serving):

Calories: 203; Fat: 8.9g; Sodium: 340mg; Carbs: 7.2g; Fiber: 1.2g; Sugar: 11.3g; Protein: 5.3g

Cheese and Fried Egg Sandwich

Prep Time: 15 Minutes   Cook Time: 15 Minutes   Serves: 4

Preparation and Cooking Tips: Enjoy sauteed veggies on the side for a change of taste.

Serving Suggestion: Serve the sandwich with a cauliflower bacon salad on the side.

Ingredients:

- 8 slices white bread, cut into 4 inches round
- 4 slices processed American cheese
- 2 tablespoons mayonnaise
- 2 tablespoons ketchup
- 2 teaspoons butter
- 4 eggs
- Salt and pepper

Directions:

1. Melt butter in a suitable skillet crack one egg and cook until set. Transfer the egg to a plate and fry more eggs in the same way.
2. Mix mayonnaise with ketchup, black pepper, and salt in a bowl.
3. Preheat the Breakfast Sandwich Maker until the green PREHEAT light comes on.
4. Lift cover, top rings, and cooking plates.
5. Place a bread slice inside the bottom tray of the sandwich maker and top it with ¼ the mayonnaise on top.
6. Lower the cooking plate and top rings then place a fried egg on top.
7. Place the other bread slice on top. Cover the top hood, and let the sandwich cook for 5 minutes.
8. Rotate the handle of the cooking plate clockwise until it stops. Lift the hood, and the rings and transfer the sandwich to a plate.
9. Make more sandwiches in the same way.

Nutritional Value (Amount per Serving):

Calories: 429; Fat: 17g; Sodium: 422mg; Carbs: 5g; Fiber: 0g; Sugar: 1g; Protein: 41g

Scrambled Egg Sandwich

Prep Time: 15 Minutes   Cook Time: 7 Minutes   Serves: 1

Preparation and Cooking Tips: Add some additional cream to the filling.

Serving Suggestion: Serve the sandwich with your favorite smoothie on the side.

Ingredients:

- ¼ cup whey protein isolate
- 1 teaspoon xanthan gum
- ½ teaspoon baking powder
- 1 pinch black pepper

- ½ cup almond flour
- ½ cup egg whites
- 1 egg, scrambled
- 1 pinch salt

Directions:

1. Mix almond flour with xanthan gum, protein, baking powder, and egg whites in a 4-inch ramekin.
2. Cook this bread batter in the microwave for 2 minutes the slice into 2 equal-sized slices.
3. Preheat the Breakfast Sandwich Maker until the green PREHEAT light comes on.
4. Lift cover, top rings, and cooking plates. Place one slice of the bread in the sandwich maker.
5. Lower the cooking plate and top rings then add scrambled egg, salt, and black pepper.
6. Add the other circle of the bread on top.
7. Cover the top hood, and let the sandwich cook for 5 minutes.
8. Rotate the handle of the cooking plate clockwise until it stops.
9. Lift the hood, and the rings and transfer the sandwich to a plate.

Nutritional Value (Amount per Serving):

Calories: 361; Fat: 16g; Sodium: 515mg; Carbs: 9.3g; Fiber: 0.1g; Sugar: 18.2g; Protein: 33.3g

Egg and Spinach Sandwich

Prep Time: 15 Minutes   Cook Time: 5 Minutes   Serves: 1

Preparation and Cooking Tips: you can also add a lettuce leaf to the filling.

Serving Suggestion: Serve the sandwich with crispy sweet potato fries on the side.

Ingredients:

- 1 whole-wheat English muffin, split and toasted
- 1 teaspoon hot sauce, such as Tabasco
- 2 tablespoons pimiento cheese
- ¼ cup baby spinach
- 1 large egg, scrambled

Directions:

1. Preheat the Breakfast Sandwich Maker until the green PREHEAT light comes on.
2. Lift cover, top rings, and cooking plates.
3. Place half of the English muffin, cut-side up, inside the bottom tray of the sandwich maker.
4. Add spinach, egg, hot sauce, and cheese on top 5. Now lower the cooking plate and top rings.
6. Place the other half of the muffin on top.
7. Cover the top hood, and let the sandwich cook for 5

minutes.
8. Rotate the handle of the cooking plate clockwise until it stops.
9. Lift the hood, and the rings and transfer the sandwich to a plate.

Nutritional Value (Amount per Serving):

Calories: 380; Fat: 8g; Sodium: 339mg; Carbs: 5.6g; Fiber: 1g; Sugar: 2g; Protein: 21g

Curried Turkey Sandwich

Prep Time: 15 Minutes   Cook Time: 17 Minutes   Serves: 1

Preparation and Cooking Tips: Add some additional cheese to the filling.

Serving Suggestion: Serve the sandwich with your favorite keto salad on the side.

Ingredients:

- ½ teaspoons madras curry powder
- 1 tablespoon chopped coriander
- ¼ cup whey protein isolate
- 1 teaspoon xanthan gum
- ½ teaspoon baking powder
- ½ tablespoons sunflower oil
- ½ cup almond flour
- ¼ red onion, grated
- ½ cup egg whites
- ½ garlic clove, crushed
- 4 ounces turkey mince
- ½ egg yolk

Directions:

1. Mix almond flour with xanthan gum, protein, baking powder, and egg whites in a 4-inch ramekin. Cook this bread batter in the microwave for 2 minutes then slice it into 2 equal-sized slices.
2. Blend turkey with red onion, curry powder, coriander, garlic, and egg yolk in a food processor for 1 minute.
3. Set a suitable skillet with olive oil over medium-high heat. Make 1 patty out of the turkey mixture. Sear the turkey patty in the oil for 5 minutes per side.
4. Preheat the Breakfast Sandwich Maker until the green PREHEAT light comes on. Lift cover, top rings, and cooking plates.
5. Place a bread slice, cut-side up, inside the bottom tray of the sandwich maker.
6. Lower the cooking plate and top rings then place a patty.
7. Place the other half of the bun on top. Cover the top hood, and let the sandwich cook for 5 minutes.
8. Rotate the handle of the cooking plate clockwise

until it stops. Lift the hood, and the rings and transfer the sandwich to a plate.

9. Repeat the same steps with the remaining ingredients.

Nutritional Value (Amount per Serving):

Calories: 361; Fat: 16g; Sodium: 515mg; Carbs: 9.3g; Fiber: 0.1g; Sugar: 18.2g; Protein: 33.3g

Sausage and Cheddar Sandwich

Prep Time: 15 Minutes   Cook Time: 9 Minutes   Serves: 1

Preparation and Cooking Tips: You can also add lettuce leaves to the filling.

Serving Suggestion: Serve the sandwich with crispy bacon and your favorite sauce on the side.

Ingredients:

- 1 (0.5-ounces) slice cracker-cuts sharp Cheddar cheese
- 1 (1.2-ounces) fully cooked turkey sausage patty
- ¼ teaspoon fresh Italian parsley, chopped
- ¼ teaspoon fresh basil, chopped
- 2 large egg
- Salt and black pepper

Directions:

1. Beat the egg with black pepper, basil, salt, and parsley in a small bowl.
2. Set a pan with two 4-inch metal rings in it.
3. Pour half of the prepared egg mixture into each ring and cook for 2 minutes per side.
4. Preheat the Breakfast Sandwich Maker until the green PREHEAT light comes on.
5. Lift cover, top rings, and cooking plates. Place one-half of the egg in the sandwich maker.
6. Lower the cooking plate and top rings then add sausage patty and cheddar cheese.
7. Place the other top half of the egg circle on top. Cover the top hood, and let the sandwich cook for 5 minutes.
8. When finished cooking, rotate the handle of the cooking plate clockwise until it stops.
9. Lift the hood, and the rings and transfer the sandwich to a plate.

Nutritional Value (Amount per Serving):

Calories: 245; Fat: 14g; Sodium: 122mg; Carbs: 8g; Fiber: 1.2g; Sugar: 12g; Protein: 4.3g

Buttery Cheese and Egg Bagel

Prep Time: 15 Minutes   Cook Time: 5 Minutes   Serves: 1

Preparation and Cooking Tips: Add some additional ground black pepper to the filling.

Serving Suggestion: Serve the sandwich with crispy bacon and your favorite sauce on the side.

Ingredients:

- 1 slice of American cheese
- 1 plain bagel, sliced
- 1 pat of butter
- 1 egg

Directions:

1. Preheat the Breakfast Sandwich Maker until the green PREHEAT light comes on.
2. Lift cover, top rings, and cooking plates.
3. Place the lower half of the bagel in the sandwich maker and top with butter.
4. Place the slice of American cheese on top of the bagel bottom.
5. Now lower the cooking plate and top rings, then pour in the egg.
6. Cover the top hood, and let the sandwich cook for 5 minutes.
7. When finished cooking, rotate the handle of the cooking plate clockwise until it stops.
8. Lift the hood, and the rings and transfer the sandwich to a plate.

Nutritional Value (Amount per Serving):

Calories: 316; Fat: 12.2g; Sodium: 587mg; Carbs: 12.2g; Fiber: 1g; Sugar: 1.8g; Protein: 25.8g

Bacon and Egg Sandwich with Herbs

Prep Time: 15 Minutes   Cook Time: 5 Minutes   Serves: 6

Preparation and Cooking Tips: You can also add a layer of your favorite sauce to the filling.

Serving Suggestion: Serve the sandwich with crispy bacon and your favorite sauce on the side.

Ingredients:

- 1 head riced cauliflower cooked
- 1½ cups cheddar cheese, grated
- 12 mozzarella Cheese, slices
- ⅛ teaspoon dried sage

- ⅛ teaspoon dried oregano
- 1 bacon slice, cooked
- Dash teaspoon dried thyme
- Ground black pepper   • Butter for greasing
- Fresh parsley for garnishing
- 1 egg beaten   • 1 egg

Directions:

1. At 350 degrees F, preheat your oven.
2. Blend cauliflower with dried herbs, egg, spices, and grated cheese in a blender until smooth.
3. Line a suitable baking sheet with parchment paper and divide the cauliflower mixture into 4-inch equal rounds onto the baking sheet. Bake the cauliflower circles for 5 minutes per side.
4. Preheat the Breakfast Sandwich Maker until the green PREHEAT light comes on. Lift cover, top rings, and cooking plates.
5. Place one circle of the cauliflower bread in the sandwich maker. Now lower the cooking plate and top rings then pour the egg mixture.
6. Add the bacon, cheese slice, and another circle of the bread on top and brush it with butter.
7. Cover the top hood, and let the sandwich cook for 5 minutes.
8. When finished cooking, rotate the handle of the cooking plate clockwise until it stops. Lift the hood, and the rings and transfer the sandwich to a plate. Garnish with parsley.
9. Repeat the same steps with the remaining ingredients.

Nutritional Value (Amount per Serving):

Calories: 217; Fat: 12g; Sodium: 79mg; Carbs: 8g; Fiber: 1.1g; Sugar: 18g; Protein: 5g

Zucchini Fajita Grilled Cheese Sandwich

Prep Time: 15 Minutes   Cook Time: 10 Minutes   Serves: 4

Preparation and Cooking Tips: Add a layer of sliced bell peppers for a change of taste.

Serving Suggestion: Would you please serve the sandwich with crispy fries on the side?

Ingredients:

- 8 slices white bread, cut into 4 inches round
- ½ large red onion, sliced
- 1 medium zucchini, sliced

- 2 tablespoons olive oil
- 1 teaspoon minced garlic
- 1 teaspoon coarse sea salt
- ¼ teaspoon black pepper
- ½ teaspoon cumin powder
- ¼ cup chimichurri sauce
- 8 slices mozzarella cheese
- 3 bell peppers, sliced

Directions:

1. Sauté red onion, zucchini, olive oil, garlic, sea salt, black pepper, bell peppers, and cumin powder in a skillet for 5 minutes.
2. Preheat the Breakfast Sandwich Maker until the green PREHEAT light comes on.
3. Lift cover, top rings, and cooking plates.
4. Place a bread slice inside the bottom tray of the sandwich maker.
5. Spread chimichurri sauce, zucchini mixture, and a mozzarella cheese slice on top.
6. Now lower the cooking plate and top rings. Place another bread slice on top.
7. Cover the top hood, and let the sandwich cook for 5 minutes.
8. Rotate the handle of the cooking plate clockwise until it stops.
9. Lift the hood, and the rings and transfer the sandwich to a plate.

Nutritional Value (Amount per Serving):

Calories: 334; Fat: 16g; Sodium: 462mg; Carbs: 3g; Fiber: 0.4g; Sugar: 3g; Protein: 35.3g

Avocado, Spinach, and Cheese Panini

Prep Time: 15 Minutes   Cook Time: 5 Minutes   Serves: 2

Preparation and Cooking Tips: Add some additional ground black pepper to the filling.

Serving Suggestion: Serve the sandwich with your favorite sauce on the side.

Ingredients:

- ¼ cup whey protein isolate
- 1 teaspoon xanthan gum
- ½ teaspoon baking powder
- 1 slice Colby jack cheese
- ½ cup egg whites   • 6 leaves of spinach
- ½ cup almond flour   • 2 slices tomatoes

- ½ avocado sliced

Directions:

1. Mix almond flour with xanthan gum, protein, baking powder, and egg whites in a 4-inch ramekin.
2. Cook this bread batter in the microwave for 2 minutes then slice it into 2 equal-sized slices.
3. Preheat the Breakfast Sandwich Maker until the green PREHEAT light comes on.
4. Lift cover, top rings, and cooking plates. Place the lower half of the bread in the sandwich maker.
5. Lower the cooking plate and top rings then place ½ of the fillings on top.
6. Add the other circle of the bread on top. Cover the top hood, and let the sandwich cook for 5 minutes.
7. When finished cooking, rotate the handle of the cooking plate clockwise until it stops.
8. Lift the hood, and the rings and transfer the sandwich to a plate.
9. Repeat the same steps with the remaining ingredients.

Nutritional Value (Amount per Serving):

Calories: 248; Fat: 16g; Sodium: 95mg; Carbs: 8.4g; Fiber: 0.3g; Sugar: 10g; Protein: 14.1g

Cheese and Egg Whites Muffin

Prep Time: 15 Minutes   Cook Time: 5 Minutes   Serves: 1

Preparation and Cooking Tips: You can also add a drizzle of lemon juice on top of the filling.

Serving Suggestion: Serve the sandwich with your favorite sauce on the side.

Ingredients:

- 1 whole wheat English muffin, cut in half
- 1 slice of low-fat mozzarella cheese
- 2 large eggs, egg whites only

Directions:

1. Preheat the Breakfast Sandwich Maker until the green PREHEAT light comes on.
2. Lift cover, top rings, and cooking plates.
3. Place the lower half of the muffin in the sandwich maker.
4. Place the slice of low-fat mozzarella cheese on the English muffin.
5. Next, on the egg cooking plate, add the egg whites.
6. Lower the cooking plate and top rings then pour in the egg.

7. Place another muffin half on top. Cover the top hood, and let the sandwich cook for 5 minutes.
8. When finished cooking, rotate the handle of the cooking plate clockwise until it stops.
9. Lift the hood, and the rings and transfer the sandwich to a plate.

Nutritional Value (Amount per Serving):

Calories: 336; Fat: 27.1g; Sodium: 66mg; Carbs: 1.1g; Fiber: 0.4g; Sugar: 0.2g; Protein: 19.7g

Cauliflower, Chicken, and Cranberry Sandwich

Prep Time: 15 Minutes   Cook Time: 5 Minutes   Serves: 1

Preparation and Cooking Tips: Add some additional dried herbs to the filling.

Serving Suggestion: Serve the sandwich with your favorite sauce on the side.

Ingredients:

- 1 dash teaspoon ground mustard seed
- 1 cauliflower head, riced cooked
- 2 tablespoons of dried cranberries
- 1½ cups cheddar cheese, grated
- 1 dash teaspoon dried thyme
- 12 mozzarella Cheese, slices
- ⅛ teaspoon dried sage
- ⅛ teaspoon dried oregano
- 1 teaspoon of chopped parsley
- Parsley for garnishing
- 2 teaspoons of mayonnaise
- 1 cup of cooked chicken
- Butter for greasing
- 1 egg beaten
- Black pepper, to taste

Directions:

1. At 350 degrees F, preheat your oven.
2. Blend cauliflower with dried herbs, egg, spices, and grated cheese in a blender until smooth.
3. Line a suitable baking sheet with parchment paper and divide the cauliflower mixture into 3-4-inch equal rounds onto the baking sheet. Bake the cauliflower circles for 5 minutes per side.
4. Preheat the Breakfast Sandwich Maker until the green PREHEAT light comes on. Lift cover, top rings, and cooking plates.
5. Place one circle of the cauliflower bread in the

sandwich maker. Top it with 1 mozzarella cheese slice.

6. Lower the cooking plate and top rings then place the remaining fillings.
7. Add the other circle of the bread on top and brush it with butter. Cover the top hood, and let the sandwich cook for 5 minutes.
8. When finished cooking, rotate the handle of the cooking plate clockwise until it stops. Lift the hood, and the rings and transfer the sandwich to a plate.
9. Garnish with parsley.

Nutritional Value (Amount per Serving):

Calories: 159; Fat: 3g; Sodium: 277mg; Carbs: 9g; Fiber: 1g; Sugar: 9g; Protein: 2g

Turkey, Avocado, and Cheddar Sandwich

Prep Time: 15 Minutes   Cook Time: 7 Minutes   Serves: 1

Preparation and Cooking Tips: Add some additional cream to the filling.

Serving Suggestion: Serve the sandwich with your favorite keto dip on the side.

Ingredients:

- 1½ ounces roasted turkey, shredded
- 1½ tablespoons mayonnaise
- 1 slice aged cheddar cheese
- ¼ cup whey protein isolate
- 1 teaspoon xanthan gum
- ½ teaspoon baking powder
- ½ cup almond flour   • 2 bacon slices
- ½ cup egg whites   • ¼ sliced avocado

Directions:

1. Mix almond flour with xanthan gum, protein, baking powder, and egg whites in a 4-inch ramekin.
2. Cook this bread batter in the microwave for 2 minutes the slice into 2 equal-sized slices.
3. Preheat the Breakfast Sandwich Maker until the green PREHEAT light comes on.
4. Lift cover, top rings, and cooking plates. Place a bread slice in the sandwich maker.
5. Lower the cooking plate and top rings then place turkey and other fillings on top.
6. Add the other circle of the bread on top. Cover the top hood, and let the sandwich cook for 5 minutes.
7. Rotate the handle of the cooking plate clockwise

until it stops.
8. Lift the hood, and the rings and transfer the sandwich to a plate.

Nutritional Value (Amount per Serving):

Calories: 361; Fat: 16g; Sodium: 515mg; Carbs: 9.3g; Fiber: 0.1g; Sugar: 18.2g; Protein: 33.3g

Avocado and Chicken Panini

Prep Time: 15 Minutes   Cook Time: 5 Minutes   Serves: 2

Preparation and Cooking Tips: You can also add lettuce leaves to the filling.

Serving Suggestion: Serve the sandwich with crispy bacon and your favorite sauce on the side.

Ingredients:

- ¼ cup whey protein isolate
- 1 teaspoon xanthan gum
- ½ teaspoon baking powder
- ½ cup almond flour
- 1 chicken patty, cooked
- ½ cup egg whites   • 1 cheese slices
- 1 avocado, sliced   • 1 slice tomatoes
- 1 slice ham

Directions:

1. Mix almond flour with xanthan gum, protein, baking powder, and egg whites in a 4-inch ramekin.
2. Cook this bread batter in the microwave for 2 minutes then slice into 2 equal-sized slices.
3. Preheat the Breakfast Sandwich Maker until the green PREHEAT light comes on.
4. Lift cover, top rings, and cooking plates. Place the lower half of the bread in the sandwich maker.
5. Lower the cooking plate and top rings, then place ½ of the fillings on top.
6. Add the other circle of the bread on top. Cover the top hood, and let the sandwich cook for 5 minutes.
7. When finished cooking, rotate the handle of the cooking plate clockwise until it stops.
8. Lift the hood, and the rings and transfer the sandwich to a plate.
9. Repeat the same steps with the remaining ingredients.

Nutritional Value (Amount per Serving):

Calories: 351; Fat: 19g; Sodium: 412mg; Carbs: 3g; Fiber: 0.3g; Sugar: 1g; Protein: 23g

Chapter 3: Meat Sandwiches and Burgers

Mayo Patty Melts

Prep Time: 15 Minutes   Cook Time: 15 Minutes   Serves: 3

Preparation and Cooking Tips: you can also add a lettuce leaf to the filling.

Serving Suggestion: Would you please serve the sandwich with crispy fries on the side?

Ingredients:

- 6 (1 ounce) slices white bread, cut into 4 inches round
- 2 chipotle peppers in adobo sauce, minced
- 1 chipotle pepper in adobo sauce, minced
- 6 (½ ounce) slices pepper jack cheese
- 3 tablespoons chili seasoning mix
- 1 lb. ground beef   • ¼ cup mayonnaise
- ½ fluid ounce beer

Directions:

1. Mix beef with chili seasoning mix, 2 chipotle peppers, and beer in a food processor for 1 minute.
2. Make 3 equal-sized patties out of this mixture. Sear the patties in a skillet for 5 minutes per side.
3. Preheat the Breakfast Sandwich Maker until the green PREHEAT light comes on.
4. Lift cover, top rings, and cooking plates.
5. Place one bread slice inside the bottom tray of the sandwich maker then spread ¼ mayonnaise and chipotle pepper on top.
6. Place a beef patty and a cheese slice on top of the mayo. Now lower the cooking plate and top rings.
7. Place another bread slice on top. Cover the top hood, and let the sandwich cook for 5 minutes.
8. Rotate the handle of the cooking plate clockwise until it stops. Lift the hood, and the rings and transfer the sandwich to a plate.
9. Repeat the same with the remaining ingredients.

Nutritional Value (Amount per Serving):

Calories: 419; Fat: 13g; Sodium: 432mg; Carbs: 9.1g; Fiber: 3g; Sugar: 1g; Protein: 33g

Mayo Gourmet Pork Sandwich

Prep Time: 15 Minutes   Cook Time: 5 Minutes   Serves: 1

Preparation and Cooking Tips: You can also add a drizzle of paprika on top of the filling.

Serving Suggestion: Serve the sandwich with crispy bacon and your favorite sauce on the side.

Ingredients:

- 2 sliced Gardenia loaf bread, cut into a 4-inch circle
- 3 tablespoons mayonnaise
- ⅛ piece red bell pepper, sliced
- 4 pounds pork strips   • Choice of greens

Directions:

1. Cook pork strips and bell peppers in a skillet until tender.
2. Preheat the Breakfast Sandwich Maker until the green PREHEAT light comes on.
3. Lift cover, top rings, and cooking plates.
4. Place one bread slice in the sandwich maker and spread mayonnaise on top.
5. Lower the cooking plate and top rings then place ¼ cup pork, peppers, and greens on top.
6. Add another bread slice on top. Cover the top hood, and let the sandwich cook for 5 minutes.
7. When finished cooking, rotate the handle of the cooking plate clockwise until it stops.
8. Lift the hood, and the rings and transfer the sandwich to a plate.
9. Repeat the same steps with the remaining ingredients.

Nutritional Value (Amount per Serving):

Calories: 336; Fat: 6g; Sodium: 181mg; Carbs: 1.3g; Fiber: 0.2g; Sugar: 0.4g; Protein: 69.2g

Mayo Roasted Beef Muffin Sandwiches

Prep Time: 15 Minutes   Cook Time: 5 Minutes   Serves: 6

Preparation and Cooking Tips: You can also add lettuce leaves to the filling.

Serving Suggestion: Serve the sandwich with crispy bacon and your favorite sauce on the side.

Ingredients:

- ¼ cup plus 2 tablespoons jarred grated horseradish (with liquid)
- 24 ounces freshly sliced rare roast beef
- 1 tablespoon, plus 2 teaspoons salt
- 6 tablespoons red wine vinegar
- ½ teaspoon grated lemon zest
- Freshly ground black pepper
- 6 English muffins, cut in half
- 12 slices ripened tomatoes

- 3 cups watercress or arugula
- 1 red onion, sliced thinly   • ¾ cup sour cream
- ¾ cup mayonnaise   • Hot sauce

Directions:

1. In a small bowl, mix onion and 1 tablespoon salt. Set aside for 20 minutes.
2. Rinse the onions with cold running water. Drain and squeeze to remove excess liquid. Combine the onions and the vinegar and marinate for at least 30 minutes or up to 24 hours.
3. In a small bowl, mix the mayonnaise, hot sauce, black pepper, horseradish, zest, sour cream, and 2 teaspoons salt. Then refrigerate the horseradish sauce for 30 minutes at least.
4. Preheat the Breakfast Sandwich Maker until the green PREHEAT light comes on. Lift cover, top rings, and cooking plates.
5. Place the lower half of a muffin in the sandwich maker. Top it with ⬜ of the filling ingredients except beef.
6. Lower the cooking plate and top rings then place the ⬜ th of the beef on top.
7. Place the other top half of a muffin on top. Cover the top hood, and let the sandwich cook for 5 minutes.
8. When finished cooking, rotate the handle of the cooking plate clockwise until it stops. Lift the hood, and the rings and transfer the sandwich to a plate.
9. Repeat the same with the remaining ingredients.

Nutritional Value (Amount per Serving):

Calories: 260; Fat: 16g; Sodium: 585mg; Carbs: 3.1g; Fiber: 1.3g; Sugar: 0.2g; Protein: 25.5g

Homemade St. Patty's Melts

Prep Time: 15 Minutes   Cook Time: 12 Minutes   Serves: 4

Preparation and Cooking Tips: Add a layer of sliced bell peppers for a change of taste.

Serving Suggestion: Serve the sandwich with a cauliflower bacon salad on the side.

Ingredients:

- ¾ cup sliced green onions, white and light green parts only
- 8 thick slices of French bread, cut into 4 inches round
- 1 (8 ounces) package of Irish white cheddar cheese, sliced

- 1 pinch cayenne pepper, or to taste
- 2 tablespoons seasoned rice vinegar
- 1 bunch Lacinato kale
- 1 bunch of mustard greens
- 10 tablespoons Irish butter
- 2 garlic cloves, minced   • Salt and black pepper

Directions:

1. Sauté kale with greens, garlic, green onions, black pepper, butter, salt cayenne pepper, and rice vinegar in a skillet for 7 minutes.
2. Preheat the Breakfast Sandwich Maker until the green PREHEAT light comes on.
3. Lift cover, top rings, and cooking plates. Place one bread slice inside the bottom tray of the sandwich maker.
4. Lower the cooking plate and top rings, then add ¼ of the kale mixture.
5. Place a cheese slice and the other bread slice on top.
6. Cover the top hood, and let the sandwich cook for 5 minutes.
7. Rotate the handle of the cooking plate clockwise until it stops.
8. Lift the hood, and the rings and transfer the sandwich to a plate.
9. Repeat the same step with the remaining ingredients.

Nutritional Value (Amount per Serving):

Calories: 361; Fat: 16g; Sodium: 189mg; Carbs: 3g; Fiber: 0.3g; Sugar: 18.2g; Protein: 33.3g

Awesome Patty Melts

Prep Time: 15 Minutes   Cook Time: 15 Minutes   Serves: 4

Preparation and Cooking Tips: Add a layer of pickled onions for a change of taste.

Serving Suggestion: Would you please serve the sandwich with a broccoli salad on the side?

Ingredients:

- 2 garlic cloves, minced, or more to taste
- 8 slices rye bread, cut into 4 inches round
- 1 tablespoon Worcestershire sauce
- 3 tablespoons unsalted butter
- ½ teaspoon black pepper
- 4 slices cheddar cheese
- 4 teaspoons Dijon mustard
- 1 lb. ground sirloin   • 3 tablespoons olive oil

- 2 medium onions, sliced
- Cooking spray
- ½ teaspoon salt

Directions:

1. Mix beef with black pepper, butter, salt, garlic, and Worcestershire sauce in a food processor for 1 minute.
2. Make 4 equal-sized patties out of this mixture. Sear the patties in a skillet with oil for 5 minutes per side.
3. Preheat the Breakfast Sandwich Maker until the green PREHEAT light comes on.
4. Lift cover, top rings, and cooking plates.
5. Place one bread slice inside the bottom tray of the sandwich maker then spread 1 teaspoon mustard on top.
6. Place a beef patty and a cheese slice on top of the mustard. Now lower the cooking plate and top rings.
7. Place another bread slice on top. Cover the top hood, and let the sandwich cook for 5 minutes.
8. Rotate the handle of the cooking plate clockwise until it stops. Lift the hood, and the rings and transfer the sandwich to a plate.
9. Repeat the same with the remaining ingredients.

Nutritional Value (Amount per Serving):

Calories: 384; Fat: 25g; Sodium: 460mg; Carbs: 6g; Fiber: 0.4g; Sugar: 2g; Protein: 26g

Worcestershire Cheddar and Beef Sandwich

Prep Time: 15 Minutes   Cook Time: 5 Minutes   Serves: 4

Preparation and Cooking Tips: You can also add a layer of your favorite sauce to the filling.

Serving Suggestion: Serve the sandwich with crispy bacon and your favorite sauce on the side.

Ingredients:

- 1-pound loaf of French or Italian-style bread, cut into a 4-inch circle
- 1 green bell pepper, sliced in rings
- 1 teaspoon Worcestershire sauce
- 2 tablespoons butter, softened
- 1 cup shredded Cheddar cheese
- ¼ cup minced green onions
- ⅛ teaspoon garlic powder
- 1-pound ground beef
- 2 tomatoes, sliced
- 1 cup sour cream
- 1 tablespoon milk
- ¾ teaspoon salt

Directions:

1. Fry your beef and onions and remove any excess oils.
2. Now add milk, salt, pepper, garlic, Worcestershire sauce, garlic, and sour cream.
3. Preheat the Breakfast Sandwich Maker until the green PREHEAT light comes on.
4. Lift cover, top rings, and cooking plates. Place one bread slice in the sandwich maker then add ¼ of the butter on top.
5. Now lower the cooking plate and top rings then add ¼ of the rest of the fillings.
6. Place another bread slice on top. Cover the top hood, and let the sandwich cook for 5 minutes.
7. When finished cooking, rotate the handle of the cooking plate clockwise until it stops.
8. Lift the hood, and the rings and transfer the sandwich to a plate.
9. Repeat the same steps with the remaining ingredients.

Nutritional Value (Amount per Serving):

Calories: 354; Fat: 7.9g; Sodium: 704mg; Carbs: 6g; Fiber: 3.6g; Sugar: 6g; Protein: 18g

Fried Mushroom and Beef Sandwich

Prep Time: 15 Minutes   Cook Time: 5 Minutes   Serves: 4

Preparation and Cooking Tips: Add some additional dried herbs to the filling.

Serving Suggestion: Serve the sandwich with your favorite sauce on the side.

Ingredients:

- 1 loaf of hearty country bread, cut into 4-inch circle
- 3-pound boneless beef round steak, 2 inches thick
- 2 cups sliced fresh mushrooms
- 3 tablespoons vegetable oil
- 1 garlic clove, minced
- Garlic salt to taste
- 1 onion, sliced
- Salt and ground black pepper

Directions:

1. Fry your steak in 1 tablespoon of veggie oil for 6 minutes per side then place the steak to the side.
2. Stir fry your mushrooms, onions, and garlic for 7 minutes until the onions are see-through in 2 more

tablespoons of veggie oil.

3. Preheat the Breakfast Sandwich Maker until the green PREHEAT light comes on.
4. Lift cover, top rings, and cooking plates. Place one bread slice in the sandwich maker then add butter on top.
5. Now lower the cooking plate and top rings then add ¼ of the rest of the fillings.
6. Place another bread slice on top. Cover the top hood, and let the sandwich cook for 5 minutes.
7. When finished cooking, rotate the handle of the cooking plate clockwise until it stops.
8. Lift the hood, and the rings and transfer the sandwich to a plate.
9. Repeat the same steps with the remaining ingredients.

Nutritional Value (Amount per Serving):

Calories: 305; Fat: 15g; Sodium: 482mg; Carbs: 17g; Fiber: 3g; Sugar: 2g; Protein: 35g

Cheese, Corned Beef, and Sauerkraut Sandwich

Prep Time: 15 Minutes   Cook Time: 5 Minutes   Serves: 4

Preparation and Cooking Tips: Add some additional dried herbs to the filling.

Serving Suggestion: Serve the sandwich with your favorite sauce on the side.

Ingredients:

- 4 slices deli sliced corned beef
- ½ cup drained sauerkraut
- 4 English muffins, sliced   • 4 slices cheese
- 1 tablespoon butter   • ¼ cup dressing

Directions:

1. Preheat the Breakfast Sandwich Maker until the green PREHEAT light comes on.
2. Lift cover, top rings, and cooking plates.
3. Place the lower half of the muffin in the sandwich maker.
4. Top the muffin with ¼ of the butter, cheese, sauerkraut.
5. Lower the cooking plate and top rings then top it with ¼ beef and pour in the ¼ dressing.
6. Cover the top hood, and let the sandwich cook for 5 minutes.
7. When finished cooking, rotate the handle of the

cooking plate clockwise until it stops.
8. Lift the hood, and the rings and transfer the sandwich to a plate.
9. Repeat the same with the remaining ingredients.

Nutritional Value (Amount per Serving):

Calories: 266; Fat: 6.3g; Sodium: 193mg; Carbs: 39.1g; Fiber: 7.2g; Sugar: 5.2g; Protein: 14.8g

Classic Cabbage Burgers

Prep Time: 15 Minutes   Cook Time: 25 Minutes   Serves: 8

Preparation and Cooking Tips: Add a layer of spicy mayo and pickled veggies for a change of taste.

Serving Suggestion: Serve the sandwich with crispy sweet potato fries on the side.

Ingredients:

- ½ large head of cabbage, chopped
- 1 tablespoon butter, melted
- ½ large onion, chopped   • 1 lb. ground beef
- 1 garlic clove, chopped   • 4 teaspoons water
- 8 English muffins   • Salt and black pepper

Directions:

1. Sauté beef with black pepper, onion, butter, chopped clove, and salt in a skillet for 10 minutes.
2. Stir in cabbage and water then cook on low heat for 10 minutes. Remove this beef and cabbage mixture and keep it aside.
3. Preheat the Breakfast Sandwich Maker until the green PREHEAT light comes on.
4. Lift cover, top rings, and cooking plates.
5. Place half of the English muffin, cut-side up, inside the bottom tray of the sandwich maker.
6. Lower the cooking plate and top rings, then add ⅛ of the beef mixture.
7. Place the other half of the muffin on top. Cover the top hood, and let the burger cook for 5 minutes.
8. Rotate the handle of the cooking plate clockwise until it stops. Lift the hood, and the rings and transfer the burger to a plate.
9. Repeat the same steps with the remaining muffins and ingredients.

Nutritional Value (Amount per Serving):

Calories: 418; Fat: 22g; Sodium: 350mg; Carbs: 2.2g; Fiber: 0.7g; Sugar: 1g; Protein: 24.3g

Beef Slaw and Coleslaw Sandwiches

Prep Time: 15 Minutes   Cook Time: 5 Minutes   Serves: 4

Preparation and Cooking Tips: You can also add lettuce leaves to the filling.

Serving Suggestion: Serve the sandwich with your favorite sauce on the side.

Ingredients:

- 8 slices rye bread, cut into 4-inch circle
- 10 ounces deli corned beef (thinly sliced)
- 5 slices deli Swiss cheese
- ⅓ cup salad dressing   • 1½ cup deli coleslaw

Directions:

1. Preheat the Breakfast Sandwich Maker until the green PREHEAT light comes on.
2. Lift cover, top rings, and cooking plates.
3. Place one bread slice in the sandwich maker then top it with ¼ the coleslaw.
4. Lower the cooking plate and top rings then place ¼ beef, cheese, and dressing on top.
5. Add another bread slice on top.
6. Cover the top hood, and let the sandwich cook for 5 minutes.
7. When finished cooking, rotate the handle of the cooking plate clockwise until it stops.
8. Lift the hood, and the rings and transfer the sandwich to a plate.
9. Repeat the same steps with the remaining ingredients.

Nutritional Value (Amount per Serving):

Calories: 354; Fat: 7.9g; Sodium: 704mg; Carbs: 6g; Fiber: 3.6g; Sugar: 6g; Protein: 18g

Pork Rib Muffin Sandwich

Prep Time: 15 Minutes   Cook Time: 4 hrs. 40 Minutes
Serves: 4

Preparation and Cooking Tips: Add some additional ground black pepper to the filling.

Serving Suggestion: Serve the sandwich with coleslaw and your favorite sauce on the side.

Ingredients:

- 18 ounces bottle of barbeque sauce
- 3 pounds of boneless pork ribs
- 14 ounces beef broth   • 4 English muffins

Directions:

1. Add pork and beef broth into the crock pot. For 4 hours let the pork cook on High.
2. After the cooking time has elapsed break up the pork with a large fork.
3. Transfer the pork to a large pot then add in your BBQ sauce and cook for almost 35 minutes. Shred the cooked pork with a fork and keep it aside.
4. Preheat the Breakfast Sandwich Maker until the green PREHEAT light comes on.
5. Lift cover, top rings, and cooking plates. Place the lower half of a muffin in the sandwich maker.
6. Now lower the cooking plate and top rings then add ½ cup shredded pork on top.
7. Place another muffin half on top. Cover the top hood, and let the sandwich cook for 5 minutes.
8. When finished cooking, rotate the handle of the cooking plate clockwise until it stops. Lift the hood, and the rings and transfer the sandwich to a plate.
9. Repeat the same steps with the remaining ingredients.

Nutritional Value (Amount per Serving):

Calories: 399; Fat: 16g; Sodium: 537mg; Carbs: 28g; Fiber: 3g; Sugar: 10g; Protein: 35g

Philly Steak Sandwich

Prep Time: 15 Minutes   Cook Time: 15 Minutes   Serves: 2

Preparation and Cooking Tips: you can also add a lettuce leaf to the filling.

Serving Suggestion: Would you please serve the sandwich with crispy carrot chips on the side?

Ingredients:

- 1 lb. beef sirloin, cut into thin 2-inch strips
- 4 hamburger buns, split lengthwise
- 1 green bell pepper, julienned
- 3 ounces Swiss cheese, sliced
- ½ teaspoon black pepper
- ½ teaspoon paprika
- ½ teaspoon chili powder
- ½ teaspoon onion powder
- ½ teaspoon garlic powder
- ½ teaspoon dried thyme
- ½ teaspoon dried marjoram
- ½ teaspoon dried basil
- 3 tablespoons vegetable oil
- ½ teaspoon salt   • 1 onion, sliced

Directions:

1. Sauté beef with all the spices, oil, herbs, onion, and bell pepper in a skillet for 10 minutes.
2. Preheat the Breakfast Sandwich Maker until the green PREHEAT light comes on.
3. Lift cover, top rings, and cooking plates.
4. Place half of a bun, cut-side up, inside the bottom tray of the sandwich maker.
5. Lower the cooking plate and top rings then add ¼ of the beef mixture.
6. Place the cheese and other top half of a bun on top. Cover the top hood, and let the sandwich cook for 5 minutes.
7. Rotate the handle of the cooking plate clockwise until it stops.
8. Lift the hood, and the rings and transfer the sandwich to a plate.
9. Repeat the same steps with the remaining ingredients.

Nutritional Value (Amount per Serving):

Calories: 401; Fat: 7g; Sodium: 269mg; Carbs: 5g; Fiber: 4g; Sugar: 12g; Protein: 26g

Carrot and Beef Sandwich

Prep Time: 15 Minutes   Cook Time: 5 Minutes   Serves: 2

Preparation and Cooking Tips: Add some additional ground black pepper to the filling.

Serving Suggestion: Serve the sandwich with coleslaw and your favorite sauce on the side.

Ingredients:

- 2 sesame seed buns, toasted until the broiler
- ⅛ teaspoons ground black pepper
- 1 cup chopped cooked beef
- 2 stalks celery, chopped
- ¼ cup chopped onion
- 3 tablespoons mayonnaise
- ⅛ teaspoons garlic powder
- ¼ teaspoons salt   • 2 eggs
- 1 carrot, diced

Directions:

1. In a bowl, combine garlic powder, beef, black pepper, celery, salt, carrots, mayonnaise and onion. Mix well.
2. Preheat the Breakfast Sandwich Maker until the green PREHEAT light comes on.

3. Lift cover, top rings, and cooking plates.
4. Place the lower half of the muffin in the sandwich maker and top with ½ of the remaining fillings.
5. Lower the cooking plate and top rings, then pour in ½ of the egg.
6. Add another bun half on top. Cover the top hood, and let the sandwich cook for 5 minutes.
7. When finished cooking, rotate the handle of the cooking plate clockwise until it stops.
8. Lift the hood, and the rings and transfer the sandwich to a plate. Enjoy toasted sesame seed buns.
9. Repeat the same steps with the remaining ingredients.

Nutritional Value (Amount per Serving):

Calories: 308; Fat: 24g; Sodium: 715mg; Carbs: 0.8g; Fiber: 0.1g; Sugar: 0.1g; Protein: 21.9g

Pineapple and Bacon Sandwich

Prep Time: 15 Minutes   Cook Time: 5 Minutes   Serves: 4

Preparation and Cooking Tips: You can also add lettuce leaves to the filling.

Serving Suggestion: Serve the sandwich with your favorite sauce on the side.

Ingredients:

- 8 slices toasted white bread, cut into a 4-inch circle
- 20 ounces sliced pineapple, drained
- 8 slices Cheddar cheese • 16 bacon slices

Directions:

1. Preheat the Breakfast Sandwich Maker until the green PREHEAT light comes on.
2. Lift cover, top rings, and cooking plates.
3. Place one of the bread slices in the sandwich maker.
4. Top it with a cheese slice and bacon.
5. Lower the cooking plate and top rings then place ¼ of the pineapple slice on top.
6. Place another bread slice on top. Cover the top hood, and let the sandwich cook for 5 minutes.
7. When finished cooking, rotate the handle of the cooking plate clockwise until it stops.
8. Lift the hood, and the rings and transfer the sandwich to a plate.
9. Repeat the same with the remaining ingredients.

Nutritional Value (Amount per Serving):

Calories: 348; Fat: 30g; Sodium: 660mg; Carbs: 5g; Fiber: 0g; Sugar: 0g; Protein: 14g

Simple Patty Melt

Prep Time: 15 Minutes   Cook Time: 15 Minutes   Serves: 3

Preparation and Cooking Tips: Add a layer of pickled veggies for a change of taste.

Serving Suggestion: Serve the sandwich with crispy zucchini fries on the side.

Ingredients:

- 6 slices rye bread, cut into 4 inches round
- ¼ teaspoon ground black pepper
- 6 slices sharp cheddar cheese
- 1 lb. ground beef
- ½ teaspoon salt
- 6 teaspoons mayonnaise
- 2 tablespoons butter
- 1 large onion, sliced

Directions:

1. Mix beef with salt, black pepper, butter, and onion in a food processor for 1 minute.
2. Make 6 equal-sized patties out of this mixture. Sear the patties in a skillet for 5 minutes per side.
3. Preheat the Breakfast Sandwich Maker until the green PREHEAT light comes on.
4. Lift cover, top rings, and cooking plates.
5. Place one bread slice inside the bottom tray of the sandwich maker then spread 1 teaspoon mayonnaise on top.
6. Place a beef patty and a cheese slice on top of the mayo. Now lower the cooking plate and top rings.
7. Place another bread slice on top. Cover the top hood, and let the sandwich cook for 5 minutes.
8. Rotate the handle of the cooking plate clockwise until it stops. Lift the hood, and the rings and transfer the sandwich to a plate.
9. Repeat the same with the remaining ingredients.

Nutritional Value (Amount per Serving):

Calories: 445; Fat: 7.9g; Sodium: 581mg; Carbs: 4g; Fiber: 2.6g; Sugar: 0.1g; Protein: 42.5g

Steak and Cheese Sandwich

Prep Time: 15 Minutes   Cook Time: 15 Minutes   Serves: 4

Preparation and Cooking Tips: you can also add a lettuce leaf to the filling.

Serving Suggestion: Would you please serve the sandwich with crispy fries on the side?

Ingredients:

- 8 (1 ounce) slices of provolone cheese
- 1 large onion, sliced and quartered
- 1 tablespoon parmesan cheese
- ½ teaspoon Worcestershire sauce
- ½ teaspoon Italian seasoning
- 4 hamburger buns, split
- 2 lbs. round steak, sliced
- ½ cup mayonnaise
- 1 pinch of coarse sea salt
- 3 garlic cloves, minced
- ⅛ teaspoon liquid smoke
- 3 tablespoons olive oil

Directions:

1. Sauté steak slices with onion, garlic, smoke, Italian seasoning, oil, salt, and Worcestershire sauce for 10 minutes.
2. Preheat the Breakfast Sandwich Maker until the green PREHEAT light comes on.
3. Lift cover, top rings, and cooking plates.
4. Place half of a bun, cut-side up, inside the bottom tray of the sandwich maker.
5. Now lower the cooking plate and top rings, then add ¼ beef and the remaining ingredients on top.
6. Place the other half of the bun on top. Cover the top hood, and let the sandwich cook for 5 minutes.
7. Rotate the handle of the cooking plate clockwise until it stops.
8. Lift the hood, and the rings and transfer the sandwich to a plate.
9. Repeat the same with the remaining ingredients.

Nutritional Value (Amount per Serving):

Calories: 335; Fat: 25g; Sodium: 122mg; Carbs: 3g; Fiber: 0.4g; Sugar: 1g; Protein: 33g

Chicken Sandwich with Maple Bourbon Syrup

Prep Time: 15 Minutes   Cook Time: 15 Minutes   Serves: 2

Preparation and Cooking Tips: Add a layer of pickled onions for a change of taste.

Serving Suggestion: Serve the sandwich with a cauliflower bacon salad on the side.

Ingredients:

Fried chicken:
- 1-pound chicken cutlets, sliced in half

- 1½ cups all-purpose flour
- 2 teaspoons garlic powder
- 1 tablespoon hot sauce
- 1 teaspoon paprika
- Kosher salt and Black pepper, to taste
- Vegetable oil, for frying
- 1 cup buttermilk

Waffles:
- 4 tablespoons melted butter
- 2 boxes of cornbread mix
- ½ cup all-purpose flour
- ½ teaspoon baking soda
- 2 tablespoons honey
- 3 large eggs
- 1 cup milk

Maple bourbon syrup:
- 8 ounces pure maple syrup
- 2 ounces bourbon whisky
- 3 tablespoons butter

Directions:

1. Whisk maple syrup with butter and bourbon whisky in a bowl.
2. Mix chicken with butter, milk, and hot sauce in a bowl. Cover and refrigerate for 30 minutes for marination.
3. Mix all the waffle ingredients in a bowl until smooth. Set up a mini waffle maker pour in a small dollop of this batter and cook as per the machine's instructions. Make more small round waffles with the remaining batter and keep them aside.
4. Mix flour with garlic powder, salt, and paprika in a bowl. Coat the chicken with this flour mixture and shake off the extra. Set a deep frying pan on medium-high heat and add oil to heat. Fry the coated chicken until golden brown then transfer to a plate using a slotted.
5. Preheat the Breakfast Sandwich Maker until the green PREHEAT light comes on. Lift cover, top rings, and cooking plates. Place one mini waffle inside the bottom tray of the sandwich maker.
6. Lower the cooking plate and top rings then place a chicken cutlet on top.
7. Drizzle a teaspoon of honey mixture on top and place another mini waffle on top. Cover the top hood, and let the sandwich cook for 5 minutes.
8. Rotate the handle of the cooking plate clockwise until it stops. Lift the hood, and the rings and transfer the sandwich to a plate.
9. Repeat the same steps with the remaining ingredients.

Nutritional Value (Amount per Serving):

Calories: 357; Fat: 12g; Sodium: 48mg; Carbs: 6g; Fiber: 2g; Sugar: 0g; Protein: 24g

Provolone and Roasted Beef Sandwich

Prep Time: 16 Minutes   Cook Time: 5 Minutes   Serves: 4

Preparation and Cooking Tips: You can also add lettuce leaves to the filling.

Serving Suggestion: Serve the sandwich with crispy bacon and your favorite sauce on the side.

Ingredients:

- 1 (10.5 ounces) can beef consommé
- 1 pound sliced deli roast beef
- 8 slices provolone cheese
- 4 English muffins, split
- 1 cup water

Directions:

1. Open your buns and place them in a casserole dish.
2. Now combine water and beef consommé in a pan to make a broth. Cook your beef in this mixture for 5 minutes.
3. Preheat the Breakfast Sandwich Maker until the green PREHEAT light comes on.
4. Lift cover, top rings, and cooking plates. Place the lower half of the muffin in the sandwich maker.
5. Now lower the cooking plate and top rings, then add ¼ of the beef and cheese on top.
6. Add the other half of the muffin on top. Cover the top hood, and let the sandwich cook for 5 minutes.
7. When finished cooking, rotate the handle of the cooking plate clockwise until it stops.
8. Lift the hood, and the rings and transfer the sandwich to a plate.
9. Repeat the same steps with the remaining ingredients.

Nutritional Value (Amount per Serving):

Calories: 380; Fat: 29g; Sodium: 821mg; Carbs: 34.6g; Fiber: 0g; Sugar: 0g; Protein: 30g

Chapter 4: Poultry Sandwiches and Burgers

Bacon, Chicken, and Avocado Sandwich

Prep Time: 15 Minutes   Cook Time: 5 Minutes   Serves: 1

Preparation and Cooking Tips: Add some additional dried herbs to the filling.

Serving Suggestion: Serve the sandwich with crispy bacon and your favorite sauce on the side.

Ingredients:

- 2 ounces of grilled boneless chicken breast
- 2 pieces of fried crisp bacon
- 1 tablespoon of mayonnaise
- 2 crisp lettuce leaves
- 1 ounce of blue cheese
- 1 ounce of cream cheese
- 1 avocado
- 1 bun, split

Directions:

1. Preheat the Breakfast Sandwich Maker until the green PREHEAT light comes on.
2. Lift cover, top rings, and cooking plates.
3. Place the lower half of a bun in the sandwich maker.
4. Lower the cooking plate and top rings, then add all the fillings.
5. Place the other half of the bun on top.
6. Cover the top hood, and let the sandwich cook for 5 minutes.
7. When finished cooking, rotate the handle of the cooking plate clockwise until it stops.
8. Lift the hood, and the rings and transfer the sandwich to a plate.

Nutritional Value (Amount per Serving):

Calories: 310; Fat: 6.9g; Sodium: 296mg; Carbs: 18.7g; Fiber: 0.3g; Sugar: 1.5g; Protein: 30.2g

Chipotle Avocado and Turkey Sliders

Prep Time: 15 Minutes   Cook Time: 25 Minutes   Serves: 3

Preparation and Cooking Tips: Add a layer of pickled onions for a change of taste.

Serving Suggestion: Serve the sandwich with crispy sweet potato fries on the side.

Ingredients:

- 6 ripe baby avocados, halved, pitted and peeled
- 2 Roma tomatoes, cut into 6 slices each
- 3 leaves green-leaf lettuce, halved
- ¾ teaspoon ground chipotle pepper
- ½ teaspoon sesame seeds
- 1 lb. lean ground turkey
- ¼ cup chopped fresh cilantro
- 2 teaspoons ground cumin
- 6 teaspoons mayonnaise
- 1 small red onion, sliced
- ½ cup white vinegar
- 2 teaspoons sugar
- ½ cup water
- ¾ teaspoon salt

Directions:

1. Blend turkey with onion, sugar, white vinegar, cilantro, cumin, salt, and chipotle pepper in a food processor for 1 minute.
2. Set a suitable skillet with olive oil over medium-high heat. Make 3 equal-sized patties out of the turkey mixture. Sear the turkey patties in the oil for 5 minutes per side then transfer them to a plate.
3. Mash avocado in a bowl, drop ⅙ of the mash into the skillet, spread it into a 4-inch round, and cook for 3 minutes per side. Make more pancakes in the same way.
4. Preheat the Breakfast Sandwich Maker until the green PREHEAT light comes on.
5. Lift cover, top rings, and cooking plates. Place an avocado cake inside the bottom tray of the sandwich maker then add 1 teaspoon mayo.
6. Lower the cooking plate and top rings then place a patty, a lettuce leaf, and a tomato slice on top.
7. Place another avocado pancake on top. Cover the top hood, and let the sandwich cook for 5 minutes.
8. Rotate the handle of the cooking plate clockwise until it stops. Lift the hood, and the rings and transfer the sandwich to a plate. Sprinkle with sesame seeds.
9. Repeat the same steps with the remaining ingredients.

Nutritional Value (Amount per Serving):

Calories: 282; Fat: 15g; Sodium: 526mg; Carbs: 20g; Fiber: 0.6g; Sugar: 3.3g; Protein: 16g

Mayo Turkey Burger

Prep Time: 15 Minutes   Cook Time: 15 Minutes   Serves: 6

Preparation and Cooking Tips: you can also add a lettuce leaf to the filling.

Serving Suggestion: Serve the sandwich with crispy

zucchini fries on the side.

Ingredients:

- 1 tablespoon Worcestershire sauce
- 2 tablespoons parsley, chopped
- 6 Hamburger buns, cut in half
- 1 lb. ground turkey
- 1 large egg, beaten
- 2 garlic cloves, minced
- Kosher salt, to taste
- 6 teaspoon Mayonnaise
- Black pepper, to taste
- 1 tablespoon olive oil
- 6 Lettuce leaves
- 6 tomato slices

Directions:

1. Blend turkey with egg, Worcestershire sauce, parsley, black pepper, garlic, and salt in a food processor for 1 minute.
2. Set a suitable skillet with olive oil over medium-high heat.
3. Make six equal-sized patties out of the turkey mixture. Sear the turkey patties in the oil for 5 minutes per side.
4. Preheat the Breakfast Sandwich Maker until the green PREHEAT light comes on.
5. Lift cover, top rings, and cooking plates. Place half of a bun, cut side up, inside the bottom tray of the sandwich maker.
6. Lower the cooking plate and top rings then place a patty, a lettuce leaf, and a tomato slice on top.
7. Place the other half of the bun on top. Cover the top hood, and let the sandwich cook for 5 minutes.
8. Rotate the handle of the cooking plate clockwise until it stops. Lift the hood, and the rings and transfer the sandwich to a plate.
9. Repeat the same steps with the remaining ingredients.

Nutritional Value (Amount per Serving):

Calories: 448; Fat: 13g; Sodium: 353mg; Carbs: 23g; Fiber: 0.4g; Sugar: 1g; Protein: 29g

Chicken and Broccoli Burger

Prep Time: 15 Minutes   Cook Time: 5 Minutes   Serves: 1

Preparation and Cooking Tips: Add some additional ground black pepper to the filling.
Serving Suggestion: Serve the sandwich with coleslaw and your favorite sauce on the side.

Ingredients:

- 1 can of condensed cream of mushroom soup
- 2 tablespoons of shredded Swiss cheese
- 2 white bread slices, cut into 4-inch circle
- 1 teaspoon of Worcestershire sauce
- 1 package of grilled chicken breast
- 2 tablespoons of broccoli florets
- 1 tablespoon of milk

Directions:

1. Mix broccoli floret, Swiss cheese, mushroom soup, and milk in a bowl. Top with broccoli floret mix.
2. Preheat the Breakfast Sandwich Maker until the green PREHEAT light comes on.
3. Lift cover, top rings, and cooking plates.
4. Place one bread slice in the sandwich maker.
5. Now lower the cooking plate and top rings, then add the remaining fillings on top.
6. Add the other circle of the bread on top.
7. Cover the top hood, and let the sandwich cook for 5 minutes.
8. When finished cooking, rotate the handle of the cooking plate clockwise until it stops.
9. Lift the hood, and the rings and transfer the sandwich to a plate.

Nutritional Value (Amount per Serving):

Calories: 562; Fat: 18.4g; Sodium: 388mg; Carbs: 42.3g; Fiber: 7g; Sugar: 8.9g; Protein: 52.3g

Avocado and Chicken Pita Sandwich

Prep Time: 15 Minutes   Cook Time: 5 Minutes   Serves: 1

Preparation and Cooking Tips: You can also add a layer of your favorite sauce to the filling.
Serving Suggestion: Serve the sandwich with your favorite sauce on the side.

Ingredients:

- 2 tablespoons of Monterey Jack cheese, shredded
- 1 pita bread, split, cut in 4-inch circle
- 1 teaspoon of vegetable oil
- 1 tablespoon of taco sauce
- ½ cup of cooked chicken
- ½ cup of shredded lettuce
- 1 ounce of green chilies
- 1 tablespoon of sour cream
- 1 small sliced avocado
- 1 small onion
- 1 teaspoon of lemon juice

- ¼ teaspoons of salt

Directions:

1. Sprinkle salt and lemon juice on avocado.
2. Mix onion, chilies, oil, taco sauce, salt, and chicken.
3. Top with the avocado mix, lettuce, and cheese.
4. Preheat the Breakfast Sandwich Maker until the green PREHEAT light comes on.
5. Lift cover, top rings, and cooking plates. Place one bread round in the sandwich maker.
6. Now lower the cooking plate and top rings, then add the fillings on top.
7. Add the other circle of the bread on top. Cover the top hood, and let the sandwich cook for 5 minutes.
8. When finished cooking, rotate the handle of the cooking plate clockwise until it stops.
9. Lift the hood, and the rings and transfer the sandwich to a plate.

Nutritional Value (Amount per Serving):

Calories: 529; Fat: 17g; Sodium: 391mg; Carbs: 55g; Fiber: 6g; Sugar: 8g; Protein: 41g

Cranberry and Turkey Burgers

Prep Time: 15 Minutes   Cook Time: 15 Minutes   Serves: 4

Preparation and Cooking Tips: you can also add a lettuce leaf to the filling.

Serving Suggestion: Would you please serve the sandwich with crispy fries on the side?

Ingredients:

- ¼ cup (2 tablespoons) whole-wheat couscous
- 1 tablespoon fresh thyme, chopped
- 1½ teaspoon fresh sage, chopped
- ¼ cup dried cranberries, chopped
- 1 lb. ground turkey
- ½ cup boiling water
- 2 tablespoons olive oil
- 1 small onion, chopped
- 1 stalk celery, minced
- ½ teaspoon black pepper
- ½ teaspoon salt
- 4 buns, cut in half

Directions:

1. Boil couscous with water until soft then drain.
2. Blend turkey with couscous, celery, thyme, sage, onion, salt, black pepper, and cranberries in a food processor for 1 minute.
3. Set a suitable skillet with olive oil over medium-high heat. Make 4 equal-sized patties out of this mixture. Sear the turkey patties in the oil for 5 minutes per side.

4. Preheat the Breakfast Sandwich Maker until the green PREHEAT light comes on.
5. Lift cover, top rings, and cooking plates. Place half of a bun, cut side up, inside the bottom tray of the sandwich maker.
6. Lower the cooking plate and top rings then place a patty on top.
7. Place the other half of the bun on top. Cover the top hood, and let the sandwich cook for 5 minutes.
8. Rotate the handle of the cooking plate clockwise until it stops. Lift the hood, and the rings and transfer the sandwich to a plate.
9. Repeat the same steps with the remaining ingredients.

Nutritional Value (Amount per Serving):

Calories: 273; Fat: 22g; Sodium: 517mg; Carbs: 3.3g; Fiber: 0.2g; Sugar: 1.4g; Protein: 16.1g

Teriyaki Water Chestnut and Turkey Burger

Prep Time: 15 Minutes   Cook Time: 5 Minutes   Serves: 2

Preparation and Cooking Tips: You can also add a drizzle of paprika on top of the filling.

Serving Suggestion: Serve the sandwich with crispy bacon and your favorite sauce on the side.

Ingredients:

- 1 tablespoon of water chestnut, chopped
- 1 teaspoon of Frank's red hot sauce
- 1 teaspoon of fresh ginger, grated
- 1 tablespoon of dried breadcrumbs
- 1 tablespoon of French fried onions
- 1 tablespoon of teriyaki sauce
- ½ pound of pre-cooked turkey
- 2 sandwich buns, split
- Shredded lettuce
- 1 egg

Directions:

1. Mix water chestnut, ginger, turkey, breadcrumbs, egg, hot sauce, French fried onion, and teriyaki sauce in a bowl. Cut into 2 patties.
2. Preheat the Breakfast Sandwich Maker until the green PREHEAT light comes on.
3. Lift cover, top rings, and cooking plates. Place the lower half of a bun in the sandwich maker.
4. Lower the cooking plate and top rings, then top it with patties and half ½ of the onions, lettuce, and hot

sauce.

5. Place the other half of the bun on top.
6. Cover the top hood, and let the sandwich cook for 5 minutes.
7. When finished cooking, rotate the handle of the cooking plate clockwise until it stops.
8. Lift the hood, and the rings and transfer the sandwich to a plate.
9. Repeat the same steps with the remaining ingredients.

Nutritional Value (Amount per Serving):

Calories: 350; Fat: 19g; Sodium: 168mg; Carbs: 38g; Fiber: 6g; Sugar: 18.8g; Protein: 10g

Mayo Chicken Salad Sandwich

Prep Time: 15 Minutes   Cook Time: 5 Minutes   Serves: 1

Preparation and Cooking Tips: Add some additional dried herbs to the filling.

Serving Suggestion: Serve the sandwich with your favorite sauce on the side.

Ingredients:

- 2 multigrain bread, cut into 4-inch circle
- ⅛ teaspoons of grated lemon zest
- 1 tablespoon of plain yogurt
- 1 teaspoon of lemon juice
- 1 tablespoon of mayonnaise
- 2 pounds of chicken breast
- 1 teaspoon of fresh dill
- 2 lettuce leaves   • ⅛ teaspoons of salt

Directions:

1. Mix dill, mayonnaise, yogurt, lemon juice, salt, and lemon zest in a bowl.
2. Preheat the Breakfast Sandwich Maker until the green PREHEAT light comes on.
3. Lift cover, top rings, and cooking plates.
4. Place one bread round in the sandwich maker.
5. Lower the cooking plate and top rings, then add the lettuce leaves, chicken, and sauce on top.
6. Add the other circle of the bread on top.
7. Cover the top hood, and let the sandwich cook for 5 minutes.
8. When finished cooking, rotate the handle of the cooking plate clockwise until it stops.
9. Lift the hood, and the rings and transfer the sandwich to a plate.

Nutritional Value (Amount per Serving):

Calories: 340; Fat: 15.5g; Sodium: 404mg; Carbs: 18.3g; Fiber: 2g; Sugar: 2.7g; Protein: 30.9g

Cucumber and Turkey Pumpernickel Sandwich

Prep Time: 15 Minutes   Cook Time: 5 Minutes   Serves: 1

Preparation and Cooking Tips: You can also add a drizzle of paprika on top of the filling.

Serving Suggestion: Serve the sandwich with crispy bacon and your favorite sauce on the side.

Ingredients:

- 2 pieces of pumpernickel bread, cut into 4-inch circle
- 1½ tablespoons of non-fat mayonnaise
- ¼ teaspoons of ground black pepper
- 2 sprigs of fresh dill, chopped
- 2 slices of smoked turkey breast
- 1 teaspoon of capers   • ½ teaspoons of dried dill
- 3 thin slices of cucumber   • 1 small red onion

Directions:

1. Mix capers, mayonnaise, pepper, and dill. Top with caper mix.
2. Preheat the Breakfast Sandwich Maker until the green PREHEAT light comes on.
3. Lift cover, top rings, and cooking plates.
4. Place one bread round in the sandwich maker.
5. Now lower the cooking plate and top rings, then add the mixture and the remaining fillings on top.
6. Add the other circle of the bread on top.
7. Cover the top hood, and let the sandwich cook for 5 minutes.
8. When finished cooking, rotate the handle of the cooking plate clockwise until it stops.
9. Lift the hood, and the rings and transfer the sandwich to a plate.

Nutritional Value (Amount per Serving):

Calories: 356; Fat: 12.7g; Sodium: 293mg; Carbs: 7.9g; Fiber: 0.3g; Sugar: 7.9g; Protein: 49.5g

Spicy Turkey Burgers

Prep Time: 15 Minutes   Cook Time: 15 Minutes   Serves: 4

Preparation and Cooking Tips: Enjoy sauteed veggies on the side for a change of taste.

Serving Suggestion: Serve the sandwich with a

cauliflower bacon salad on the side.

Ingredients:

- 2 teaspoons madras curry powder
- 1 handful chopped coriander
- 1 tablespoon sunflower oil
- 4 burger buns, split in half
- 4 tablespoons mango chutney
- ½ lb. turkey mince
- ¼ red onion, grated

- 1 garlic clove, crushed
- 1 egg yolk

Directions:

1. Blend turkey with red onion, curry powder, coriander, garlic, and egg yolk in a food processor for 1 minute.
2. Set a suitable skillet with olive oil over medium-high heat.
3. Make four equal-sized patties out of the turkey mixture. Sear the turkey patties in the oil for 5 minutes per side.
4. Preheat the Breakfast Sandwich Maker until the green PREHEAT light comes on.
5. Lift cover, top rings, and cooking plates. Place half of a bun, cut side up, inside the bottom tray of the sandwich maker.
6. Spread ¼ of the mango chutney on top. Now lower the cooking plate and top rings then place a patty.
7. Place the other half of the bun on top. Cover the top hood, and let the sandwich cook for 5 minutes.
8. Rotate the handle of the cooking plate clockwise until it stops. Lift the hood, and the rings and transfer the sandwich to a plate.
9. Repeat the same steps with the remaining ingredients.

Nutritional Value (Amount per Serving):

Calories: 376; Fat: 17g; Sodium: 1127mg; Carbs: 34g; Fiber: 1g; Sugar: 3g; Protein: 29g

Turkey, Mushroom, and Swiss Cheese Burgers

Prep Time: 15 Minutes   Cook Time: 15 Minutes   Serves: 4

Preparation and Cooking Tips: you can also add a lettuce leaf to the filling.

Serving Suggestion: Serve the sandwich with crispy sweet potato fries on the side.

Ingredients:

- 2 teaspoons Worcestershire sauce

- 8 Portobello mushroom caps
- 2 tablespoons olive oil
- ¾ teaspoon black pepper
- 1 garlic clove, minced
- 1 lb. lean ground turkey
- 1 teaspoon Dijon mustard
- 4 slices Swiss cheese
- 3 cups baby arugula
- 1 small tomato, sliced
- ½ teaspoon salt

Directions:

1. Blend turkey with garlic, salt, black pepper, and Worcestershire sauce in a food processor for 1 minute.
2. Set a suitable skillet with olive oil over medium-high heat.
3. Make 4 equal-sized patties out of the turkey mixture. Sear the turkey patties in the oil for 5 minutes per side.
4. Preheat the Breakfast Sandwich Maker until the green PREHEAT light comes on. Lift cover, top rings, and cooking plates.
5. Place a Portobello mushroom cap, cut-side up, inside the bottom tray of the sandwich maker.
6. Lower the cooking plate and top rings then place a patty, of ¼ Swiss cheese, tomato, and arugula on top.
7. Place the other mushroom cap on top. Cover the top hood, and let the sandwich cook for 5 minutes.
8. Rotate the handle of the cooking plate clockwise until it stops. Lift the hood, and the rings and transfer the sandwich to a plate.
9. Repeat the same steps with the remaining ingredients.

Nutritional Value (Amount per Serving):

Calories: 321; Fat: 7.4g; Sodium: 356mg; Carbs: 29.3g; Fiber: 2.4g; Sugar: 5g; Protein: 37.2g

Cajun Chicken and Lettuce Sandwich

Prep Time: 15 Minutes   Cook Time: 5 Minutes   Serves: 1

Preparation and Cooking Tips: You can also add lettuce leaves to the filling.

Serving Suggestion: Serve the sandwich with your favorite sauce on the side.

Ingredients:

- 3 ounces of pre-cooked skinless chicken
- 1½ tablespoons of Cajun seasoning
- 1 split toasted buns
- Butter

- Lettuce
- Onion

Directions:

1. Soak chicken with Cajun seasoning.
2. Preheat the Breakfast Sandwich Maker until the green PREHEAT light comes on.
3. Lift cover, top rings, and cooking plates.
4. Place the lower half of a bun in the sandwich maker.
5. Lower the cooking plate and top rings, then add the remaining fillings.
6. Place the other half of the bun on top.
7. Cover the top hood, and let the sandwich cook for 5 minutes.
8. When finished cooking, rotate the handle of the cooking plate clockwise until it stops.
9. Lift the hood, and the rings and transfer the sandwich to a plate.

Nutritional Value (Amount per Serving):

Calories: 347; Fat: 22.3g; Sodium: 207mg; Carbs: 1.6g; Fiber: 0.3g; Sugar: 0.5g; Protein: 32.8g

Turkey Burger with Tzatziki Sauce

Prep Time: 15 Minutes   Cook Time: 15 Minutes   Serves: 6

Preparation and Cooking Tips: Add a layer of sliced bell peppers for a change of taste.

Serving Suggestion: Would you please serve the sandwich with crispy fries on the side?

Ingredients:

- 2 lbs. ground turkey
- 2 teaspoons oregano
- 4 garlic cloves, minced
- 1 small onion, grated
- ¼ cup parsley, chopped
- 1 teaspoon cumin
- 1 teaspoon black pepper
- 2 teaspoons salt
- 2 tablespoons olive oil

Burger:
- 6 romaine lettuce leaves
- 4 ounces feta, crumbled
- 6 hamburger buns, toasted
- 2 tomatoes, sliced
- 1 cup tzatziki sauce

Tzatziki sauce:
- 1 tablespoon dried dill or 2 tablespoons fresh dill
- ½ English cucumber, grated
- 1-2 garlic cloves, minced
- ½ teaspoons salt
- 1 cup Greek yogurt
- ¼ teaspoons pepper
- 2 teaspoons za'atar, optional

Directions:

1. Mix all the tzatziki sauce ingredients in a bowl and keep it aside.
2. Blend turkey with oregano, onion, parsley, cumin, garlic, black pepper, and salt in a food processor for 1 minute.
3. Set a suitable skillet with olive oil over medium-high heat. Make six equal-sized patties out of the turkey mixture. Sear the turkey patties in the oil for 5 minutes per side.
4. Preheat the Breakfast Sandwich Maker until the green PREHEAT light comes on.
5. Lift cover, top rings, and cooking plates. Place half of a bun, cut side up, inside the bottom tray of the sandwich maker.
6. Lower the cooking plate and top rings then place a patty, a lettuce leaf, a tomato slice, ⅙ feta, and tzatziki sauce on top.
7. Place the other half of the bun on top. Cover the top hood, and let the sandwich cook for 5 minutes.
8. Rotate the handle of the cooking plate clockwise until it stops. Lift the hood, and the rings and transfer the sandwich to a plate.
9. Repeat the same steps with the remaining ingredients.

Nutritional Value (Amount per Serving):

Calories: 345; Fat: 36g; Sodium: 272mg; Carbs: 41g; Fiber: 0.2g; Sugar: 0.1g; Protein: 22.5g

Herbed Onion and Chicken Burger

Prep Time: 15 Minutes   Cook Time: 15 Minutes   Serves: 8

Preparation and Cooking Tips: Add a layer of pickled onions for a change of taste.

Serving Suggestion: Would you please serve the sandwich with a broccoli salad on the side?

Ingredients:

To serve:
- 8 burger buns, split in half
- 8 bacon slices, cooked
- 8 lettuce leaves
- 1 onion, sliced
- 8 tomato slices

Burgers:
- 2 teaspoons fresh thyme, chopped
- 2 tablespoons olive oil
- ½ medium red onion, minced

- 4 garlic cloves, minced
- 2 lbs. ground chicken meat
- 1 teaspoon black pepper
- ½ cup chopped parsley
- 1 tablespoon fresh rosemary
- 1 tablespoon fresh sage
- ½ teaspoon salt

Directions:

1. Blend chicken with red onion, parsley, rosemary, garlic, salt, black pepper, sage, and thyme in a food processor for 1 minute.
2. Set a suitable skillet with olive oil over medium-high heat. Make eight equal-sized patties out of the turkey mixture. Sear the chicken patties in the oil for 5 minutes per side.
3. Preheat the Breakfast Sandwich Maker until the green PREHEAT light comes on.
4. Lift cover, top rings, and cooking plates.
5. Place half of a bun, cut-side up, inside the bottom tray of the sandwich maker.
6. Lower the cooking plate and top rings, then place a patty, an onion slice, a lettuce leaf, and a tomato slice on top.
7. Place the other half of the bun on top. Cover the top hood, and let the sandwich cook for 5 minutes.
8. Rotate the handle of the cooking plate clockwise until it stops. Lift the hood, and the rings and transfer the sandwich to a plate.
9. Repeat the same steps with the remaining ingredients.

Nutritional Value (Amount per Serving):

Calories: 457; Fat: 19g; Sodium: 557mg; Carbs: 29g; Fiber: 1.8g; Sugar: 1.2g; Protein: 32.5g

Chicken Sandwich with Tabasco Sauce

Prep Time: 15 Minutes   Cook Time: 5 Minutes   Serves: 1

Preparation and Cooking Tips: You can also add lettuce leaves to the filling.

Serving Suggestion: Serve the sandwich with crispy bacon and your favorite sauce on the side.

Ingredients:

- ½ teaspoons of Tabasco sauce
- ⅛ cup of apple cider vinegar
- ⅛ cup of jalapeno jelly   • ½ teaspoon of salt
- 1 hamburger buns   • 2 chicken breasts

Directions:

1. Mix Tabasco sauce, apple cider vinegar, jalapeno jelly, and salt in a bowl.
2. Preheat the Breakfast Sandwich Maker until the green PREHEAT light comes on.
3. Lift cover, top rings, and cooking plates.
4. Place the lower half of a bun in the sandwich maker.
5. Lower the cooking plate and top rings, then add chicken and the sauce.
6. Place the other half of the bun on top.
7. Cover the top hood, and let the sandwich cook for 5 minutes.
8. When finished cooking, rotate the handle of the cooking plate clockwise until it stops.
9. Lift the hood, and the rings and transfer the sandwich to a plate.

Nutritional Value (Amount per Serving):

Calories: 529; Fat: 38g; Sodium: 663mg; Carbs: 4g; Fiber: 1g; Sugar: 8g; Protein: 42g

Chicken Cordon Bleu Sandwich

Prep Time: 15 Minutes   Cook Time: 5 Minutes   Serves: 1

Preparation and Cooking Tips: Add some additional ground black pepper to the filling.

Serving Suggestion: Serve the sandwich with coleslaw and your favorite sauce on the side.

Ingredients:

- 1 ounce of chicken patties, cooked
- 1 slice of Swiss cheese   • Mustard
- 1 split buns   • 1 slice of ham
- 1 sliced tomato   • lettuce

Directions:

1. Preheat the Breakfast Sandwich Maker until the green PREHEAT light comes on.
2. Lift cover, top rings, and cooking plates.
3. Place the lower half of the muffin in the sandwich maker.
4. Place the lower half of a bun in the sandwich maker.
5. Lower the cooking plate and top rings, then add all the fillings.
6. Place the other half of the bun on top.
7. Cover the top hood, and let the sandwich cook for 5

minutes.

8. When finished cooking, rotate the handle of the cooking plate clockwise until it stops.
9. Lift the hood, and the rings and transfer the sandwich to a plate.

Nutritional Value (Amount per Serving):

Calories: 386; Fat: 17g; Sodium: 525mg; Carbs: 36.1g; Fiber: 2.6g; Sugar: 2.2g; Protein: 21g

Turkey and Cilantro Burgers

Prep Time: 15 Minutes   Cook Time: 15 Minutes   Serves: 2

Preparation and Cooking Tips: you can also add a lettuce leaf to the filling.

Serving Suggestion: Serve the sandwich with crispy zucchini fries on the side.

Ingredients:

- 2-inch flour tortillas, cut into 4 inches rounds
- 3 tablespoons fresh cilantro, chopped
- 2 teaspoons chilli powder
- 1 teaspoon ground cumin
- 4 slices pepper jack cheese
- 4 tablespoons sour cream
- ½ teaspoon sea salt
- ½ teaspoon black pepper
- 1 scallion, minced   • 4 green chiles
- 1 lb. ground turkey

Directions:

1. Blend turkey with cilantro, chili powder, cumin, scallion, salt, and black pepper in a food processor for 1 minute.
2. Set a suitable skillet with olive oil over medium-high heat. Make 4 equal-sized patties out of the turkey mixture. Sear the turkey patties in the oil for 5 minutes per side.
3. Preheat the Breakfast Sandwich Maker until the green PREHEAT light comes on.
4. Lift cover, top rings, and cooking plates.
5. Place a tortilla round inside the bottom tray of the sandwich maker.
6. Lower the cooking plate and top rings then place a patty, green chile, a cheese slice, and 1 tablespoon sour cream on top.
7. Place another tortilla round on top. Cover the top hood, and let the sandwich cook for 5 minutes.
8. Rotate the handle of the cooking plate clockwise

until it stops. Lift the hood, and the rings and transfer the sandwich to a plate.
9. Repeat the same steps with the remaining ingredients.

Nutritional Value (Amount per Serving):

Calories: 305; Fat: 25g; Sodium: 532mg; Carbs: 2.3g; Fiber: 0.4g; Sugar: 2g; Protein: 18.3g

Avocado and Grilled Chicken Sandwich

Prep Time: 15 Minutes   Cook Time: 5 Minutes   Serves: 2

Preparation and Cooking Tips: Add some additional ground black pepper to the filling.

Serving Suggestion: Serve the sandwich with coleslaw and your favorite sauce on the side.

Ingredients:

- ¼ cup of jalapeno pepper, sliced
- 8 ounces of grilled chicken breast
- ⅔ cup of black beans, mashed
- 1 cup of shredded lettuce
- Black pepper and salt
- 2 sandwich buns, split
- 1 ripe avocado
- 1 sliced tomato

Directions:

1. Preheat the Breakfast Sandwich Maker until the green PREHEAT light comes on.
2. Lift cover, top rings, and cooking plates.
3. Place the lower half of a bun in the sandwich maker.
4. Lower the cooking plate and top rings, then add ½ of the fillings.
5. Place the other half of the bun on top.
6. Cover the top hood, and let the sandwich cook for 5 minutes.
7. When finished cooking, rotate the handle of the cooking plate clockwise until it stops.
8. Lift the hood, and the rings and transfer the sandwich to a plate.
9. Repeat the same steps with the remaining ingredients.

Nutritional Value (Amount per Serving):

Calories: 521; Fat: 17.1g; Sodium: 840mg; Carbs: 65.5g; Fiber: 2.9g; Sugar: 2.6g; Protein: 26.1g

Sauerkraut and Turkey Sandwich

Prep Time: 15 Minutes   Cook Time: 5 Minutes   Serves: 2

Preparation and Cooking Tips: Add some additional dried herbs to the filling.

Serving Suggestion: Serve the sandwich with your favorite sauce on the side.

Ingredients:

- 4 dark rye bread slices, cut into 4-inch circle
- 4 ounces of turkey breast
- 1 tablespoon butter
- 4 ounces of sauerkraut
- 4 slices of Swiss cheese
- Salad dressing

Directions:

1. Preheat the Breakfast Sandwich Maker until the green PREHEAT light comes on.
2. Lift cover, top rings, and cooking plates.
3. Place one bread round in the sandwich maker.
4. Now lower the cooking plate and top rings, then add ½ of the fillings on top.
5. Add the other circle of the bread on top.
6. Cover the top hood, and let the sandwich cook for 5 minutes.
7. When finished cooking, rotate the handle of the cooking plate clockwise until it stops.
8. Lift the hood, and the rings and transfer the sandwich to a plate.
9. Repeat the same steps with the remaining ingredients.

Nutritional Value (Amount per Serving):

Calories: 565; Fat: 30g; Sodium: 651mg; Carbs: 20.3g; Fiber: 1.4g; Sugar: 1.7g; Protein: 53.1 g

Lemony Cheery and Chicken Sandwich

Prep Time: 15 Minutes   Cook Time: 5 Minutes   Serves: 1

Preparation and Cooking Tips: You can also add lettuce leaves to the filling.

Serving Suggestion: Serve the sandwich with your favorite sauce on the side.

Ingredients:

- 2 tablespoons of dried tart cherries
- 1 teaspoon of chopped parsley
- 2 teaspoons of mayonnaise
- 1 teaspoon of lemon juice
- 1 cup of cooked chicken
- ⅛ cup of plain yogurt
- 1 green onion
- Lettuce leaves
- 1 croissant split
- Black pepper

Directions:

1. Mix lemon juice, mayonnaise, pepper, and yogurt in a bowl.
2. Preheat the Breakfast Sandwich Maker until the green PREHEAT light comes on.
3. Lift cover, top rings, and cooking plates.
4. Place the lower half of a croissant in the sandwich maker.
5. Lower the cooking plate and top rings, then add the remaining fillings.
6. Place the other top half of the croissant on top.
7. Cover the top hood, and let the sandwich cook for 5 minutes.
8. When finished cooking, rotate the handle of the cooking plate clockwise until it stops.
9. Lift the hood, and the rings and transfer the sandwich to a plate.

Nutritional Value (Amount per Serving):

Calories: 524; Fat: 24g; Sodium: 568 mg; Carbs: 24g; Fiber: 9g; Sugar: 5.2g; Protein: 24 g

Reuben Sandwich with Swiss Cheese

Prep Time: 15 Minutes   Cook Time: 5 Minutes   Serves: 1

Preparation and Cooking Tips: You can also add lettuce leaves to the filling.

Serving Suggestion: Serve the sandwich with your favorite sauce on the side.

Ingredients:

- 1 boneless chicken breast, cooked and sliced
- 1 cup of shredded red cabbage
- ¼ cup of island salad dressing
- ½ cup of Swiss cheese
- 1 French bun, split
- 1 small onion

Directions:

1. Preheat the Breakfast Sandwich Maker until the green PREHEAT light comes on.

2. Lift cover, top rings, and cooking plates.
3. Place one bread round in the sandwich maker.
4. Top it with chicken breast slices.
5. Lower the cooking plate and top rings, then add the rest of the fillings on top.
6. Add the other circle of the bread on top.
7. Cover the top hood, and let the sandwich cook for 5 minutes.
8. When finished cooking, rotate the handle of the cooking plate clockwise until it stops.
9. Lift the hood, and the rings and transfer the sandwich to a plate.

Nutritional Value (Amount per Serving):

Calories: 525; Fat: 19g; Sodium: 230mg; Carbs: 17g; Fiber: 3.8g; Sugar: 8.5g; Protein: 67g

Basil Chicken Burger with Pizza Sauce

Prep Time: 15 Minutes   Cook Time: 5 Minutes   Serves: 2

Preparation and Cooking Tips: You can also add a drizzle of lemon juice on top of the filling.
Serving Suggestion: Serve the sandwich with crispy bacon and your favorite sauce on the side.

Ingredients:

- 4 ounces of ground chicken
- 2 slices of provolone cheese
- 1 cup of pizza sauce
- ½ teaspoon of basil   • 2 buns, split

Directions:

1. Top with 1 slice of provolone cheese, dried basil, and pizza sauce.
2. Preheat the Breakfast Sandwich Maker until the green PREHEAT light comes on.
3. Lift cover, top rings, and cooking plates.
4. Place the lower half of a bun in the sandwich maker.
5. Lower the cooking plate and top rings, then add ½ of the fillings.
6. Place the other half of the bun on top. Cover the top hood, and let the sandwich cook for 5 minutes.
7. When finished cooking, rotate the handle of the cooking plate clockwise until it stops.
8. Lift the hood, and the rings and transfer the sandwich to a plate.
9. Repeat the same steps with the remaining ingredients.

Nutritional Value (Amount per Serving):

Calories: 327; Fat: 18.3g; Sodium: 512mg; Carbs: 4.2g; Fiber: 0.5g; Sugar: 0.3g; Protein: 35.3g

Turkey Burgers with Mustard and Honey

Prep Time: 15 Minutes   Cook Time: 15 Minutes   Serves: 4

Preparation and Cooking Tips: Add a layer of pickled veggies for a change of taste.
Serving Suggestion: Serve the sandwich with crispy bacon and your favorite sauce on the side.

Ingredients:

- 4 whole-wheat hamburger buns, split
- 1 lb. ground turkey breast
- ¼ teaspoon black pepper
- ¼ cup mustard   • 4 lettuce leaves
- 2 tablespoons honey   • 4 tomato slices
- ¼ teaspoon salt   • 4 red onion slices
- 2 teaspoons canola oil

Directions:

1. Blend turkey with honey, salt, mustard, and black pepper in a food processor for 1 minute.
2. Set a suitable skillet with olive oil over medium-high heat. Make 4 equal-sized patties out of the turkey mixture. Sear the turkey patties in the oil for 5 minutes per side.
3. Preheat the Breakfast Sandwich Maker until the green PREHEAT light comes on.
4. Lift cover, top rings, and cooking plates.
5. Place half of a bun, cut-side up, inside the bottom tray of the sandwich maker.
6. Now lower the cooking plate and top rings then place a patty, a lettuce leaf, 1 onion slice, and tomato slice on top.
7. Place the other half of the bun on top. Cover the top hood, and let the sandwich cook for 5 minutes.
8. Rotate the handle of the cooking plate clockwise until it stops. Lift the hood, and the rings and transfer the sandwich to a plate.
9. Repeat the same steps with the remaining ingredients.

Nutritional Value (Amount per Serving):

Calories: 337; Fat: 20g; Sodium: 719mg; Carbs: 21g; Fiber: 0.9g; Sugar: 1.4g; Protein: 37.8g

Kentucky Turkey Sandwich

Prep Time: 15 Minutes   Cook Time: 5 Minutes   Serves: 1

Preparation and Cooking Tips: Add some additional ground black pepper to the filling.

Serving Suggestion: Serve the sandwich with coleslaw and your favorite sauce on the side.

Ingredients:

- 2 teaspoons of grated Parmesan cheese
- 2 tablespoons of cream of chicken soup
- 2 white bread slices, cut into 4-inch circle
- 1 teaspoon of lemon juice
- 2 slices of turkey breast
- 1 teaspoon of light cream
- 2 slices of bacon
- 6 mushroom caps

Directions:

1. Top with light cream, cream of chicken soup, mushrooms, and lemon juice.
2. Preheat the Breakfast Sandwich Maker until the green PREHEAT light comes on.
3. Lift cover, top rings, and cooking plates.
4. Place one bread round in the sandwich maker.
5. Now lower the cooking plate and top rings, then add the fillings on top.
6. Add the other circle of the bread on top.
7. Cover the top hood, and let the sandwich cook for 5 minutes.
8. When finished cooking, rotate the handle of the cooking plate clockwise until it stops.
9. Lift the hood, and the rings and transfer the sandwich to a plate.

Nutritional Value (Amount per Serving):

Calories: 381; Fat: 26g; Sodium: 970mg; Carbs: 10g; Fiber: 0g; Sugar: 3.7g; Protein: 26g

Chicken and Spinach Burgers

Prep Time: 15 Minutes   Cook Time: 15 Minutes   Serves: 8

Preparation and Cooking Tips: Add a layer of spicy mayo and pickled veggies for a change of taste.

Serving Suggestion: Serve the sandwich with a cauliflower bacon salad on the side.

Ingredients:

- 8 large Portobello mushrooms, cut in half horizontally
- ⅓ cup Kalamata olives, chopped
- 8 (¼ inch thick) rings of red onion
- 1 lb. ground chicken
- 1 cup chopped spinach
- 1½ teaspoon lemon zest
- 1 teaspoon garlic powder
- ½ teaspoon dried oregano
- ½ teaspoon black pepper
- 2 tablespoons olive oil
- 4 tablespoons tzatziki
- ¾ teaspoon salt
- 1 cup arugula

Directions:

1. Blend chicken with spinach, zest, garlic powder, oregano, olives, salt, and black pepper in a food processor for 1 minute.
2. Set a suitable skillet with olive oil over medium-high heat. Make 8 equal-sized patties out of the turkey mixture. Sear the chicken patties in the oil for 5 minutes per side.
3. Preheat the Breakfast Sandwich Maker until the green PREHEAT light comes on.
4. Lift cover, top rings, and cooking plates.
5. Place half of a Portobello mushroom, cut side up, inside the bottom tray of the sandwich maker.
6. Now lower the cooking plate and top rings, then place a patty, an onion ring, ⅛ of the Tzatziki, and arugula on top.
7. Place the other top half of the Portobello mushroom on top. Cover the top hood, and let the sandwich cook for 5 minutes.
8. Rotate the handle of the cooking plate clockwise until it stops. Lift the hood, and the rings and transfer the sandwich to a plate.
9. Repeat the same steps with the remaining ingredients.

Nutritional Value (Amount per Serving):

Calories: 395; Fat: 9.5g; Sodium: 655mg; Carbs: 34g; Fiber: 0.4g; Sugar: 0.4g; Protein: 28.3g

Chapter 5: Fish and Seafood Sandwiches

Salmon Burgers with Harissa Mayo

Prep Time: 15 Minutes   Cook Time: 11 Minutes   Serves: 6

Preparation and Cooking Tips: Add a layer of pickled onions for a change of taste.

Serving Suggestion: Serve the sandwich with crispy bacon and your favorite sauce on the side.

Ingredients:

Harissa mayo:
- 1 teaspoon grated lemon zest
- 1 tablespoon fresh lemon juice
- ⅔ cup mayonnaise
- ¼ cup Greek yogurt
- 2 tablespoons harissa
- Kosher salt, to taste
- Black pepper, to taste

Cumber relish:
- 1 English cucumber, sliced
- 1 tablespoon chopped dill
- 1 teaspoon kosher salt
- ⅓ cup rice vinegar
- 1 shallot, minced
- 1 teaspoon sugar

Salmon burgers:
- 1½ lbs. skinless center-cut salmon fillet, cut into cubes
- 1 small red bell pepper, chopped
- 1 small green bell pepper, chopped
- ½ cup plain dry breadcrumbs
- 1 tablespoon kosher salt
- ½ teaspoon black pepper
- 5 scallions, chopped

To cook:
- Lettuce and tomato slices, for serving
- 2 tablespoons unsalted butter
- ¼ cup olive oil
- 6 brioche buns, split

Directions:

1. Blend all the ingredients for salmon burgers in a food processor for 1 minute.
2. Mix harissa mayo ingredients in a suitable bowl. Whisk the cucumber relish ingredients in another bowl.
3. Set a pan with oil over medium heat. Make 6 patties out of the salmon mixture and sear them in the oil for 3 minutes per side.
4. Preheat the Breakfast Sandwich Maker until the green PREHEAT light comes on. Lift cover, top rings, and cooking plates.
5. Place half of a bun cut-side up, inside the bottom tray of the sandwich maker.
6. Add ⅙ of the harissa mayo, 1 salmon patty, and ⅙ of the cucumber relish on top.
7. Now lower the cooking plate and top rings. Place the other half of the bun on top. Cover the top hood, and let the sandwich cook for 5 minutes.
8. Rotate the handle of the cooking plate clockwise until it stops. Lift the hood, and the rings and transfer the sandwich to a plate Serve with the lettuce and tomato slices.
9. Repeat the same steps with the remaining ingredients.

Nutritional Value (Amount per Serving):

Calories: 425; Fat: 14g; Sodium: 411mg; Carbs: 24g; Fiber: 0.3g; Sugar: 1g; Protein: 28.3g

Tuna Salad Sandwich

Prep Time: 15 Minutes   Cook Time: 5 Minutes   Serves: 2

Preparation and Cooking Tips: You can also add a layer of your favorite sauce to the filling.

Serving Suggestion: Serve the sandwich with your favorite sauce on the side.

Ingredients:
- ¼ teaspoon lemon pepper seasoning
- 4 tablespoons mayonnaise
- 1 cup tuna flakes
- 1 tablespoon capers
- 1 teaspoon lime juice
- 1 teaspoon tarragon
- 2 burger buns, split

Directions:

1. Mix all ingredients except buns.
2. Preheat the Breakfast Sandwich Maker until the green PREHEAT light comes on.
3. Lift cover, top rings, and cooking plates.
4. Place the lower half of the muffin in the sandwich maker. Add one burger bun (bottom) inside.
5. Top with ½ of the tuna mixture. Now lower the cooking plate and top rings.
6. Place the other half of the bun on top. Cover the top hood, and let the sandwich cook for 5 minutes.
7. When finished cooking, rotate the handle of the cooking plate clockwise until it stops.
8. Lift the hood, and the rings and transfer the sandwich to a plate.
9. Repeat the same steps with the remaining

ingredients.

Nutritional Value (Amount per Serving):

Calories: 326; Fat: 13.4g; Sodium: 315mg; Carbs: 36.8g; Fiber: 5.6g; Sugar: 3.7g; Protein: 15.9g

Onion and Fish Sandwich

Prep Time: 15 Minutes   Cook Time: 5 Minutes   Serves: 2

Preparation and Cooking Tips: You can also add lettuce leaves to the filling.

Serving Suggestion: Serve the sandwich with your favorite sauce on the side.

Ingredients:

- 2 whole wheat burger buns, split in half
- 4 frozen breaded fish strips
- 2 tablespoons mayonnaise
- 1 teaspoon sweet pickle relish
- 4 slices sweet onion   • Cooking spray

Directions:

1. Spray fish strips with oil. Cook in a pan over medium heat until golden and crispy.
2. Mix mayo and sweet pickle relish in a bowl.
3. Preheat the Breakfast Sandwich Maker until the green PREHEAT light comes on.
4. Lift cover, top rings, and cooking plates.
5. Place the lower half of the muffin in the sandwich maker and add the ½ of the prepared fillings. Now lower the cooking plate and top rings.
6. Place another bun half on top. Cover the top hood, and let the sandwich cook for 5 minutes.
7. When finished cooking, rotate the handle of the cooking plate clockwise until it stops.
8. Lift the hood, and the rings and transfer the sandwich to a plate.
9. Repeat the same steps with the remaining ingredients.

Nutritional Value (Amount per Serving):

Calories: 551; Fat: 31g; Sodium: 1329mg; Carbs: 1.5g; Fiber: 0.8g; Sugar: 0.4g; Protein: 64g

Mayo Shrimp Salad Burgers

Prep Time: 15 Minutes   Cook Time: 5 Minutes   Serves: 2

Preparation and Cooking Tips: You can also add lettuce leaves to the filling.

Serving Suggestion: Serve the sandwich with crispy

bacon and your favorite sauce on the side.

Ingredients:

- 1 cup shrimp, peeled, deveined, cooked and chopped
- 1 tablespoon green onion, chopped
- 1 teaspoon Old Bay seasoning
- 4 tablespoons mayonnaise
- 1 teaspoon lemon juice   • 2 burger buns, split

Directions:

1. In a bowl, combine all the ingredients except burger buns.
2. Preheat the Breakfast Sandwich Maker until the green PREHEAT light comes on.
3. Lift cover, top rings, and cooking plates.
4. Add burger bun bottoms inside and top with ½ of the mayo mixture.
5. Spread with ½ of the shrimp mixture. Now lower the cooking plate and top rings.
6. Add the other bun half on top. Cover the top hood, and let the sandwich cook for 5 minutes.
7. When finished cooking, rotate the handle of the cooking plate clockwise until it stops.
8. Lift the hood, and the rings and transfer the sandwich to a plate.
9. Repeat the same steps with the remaining ingredients.

Nutritional Value (Amount per Serving):

Calories: 352; Fat: 9.1g; Sodium: 1294mg; Carbs: 3.9g; Fiber: 1g; Sugar: 1g; Protein: 61g

Mayo Scallop Corn Burgers

Prep Time: 15 Minutes   Cook Time: 5 Minutes   Serves: 6

Preparation and Cooking Tips: Add a layer of pickled veggies for a change of taste.

Serving Suggestion: Would you please serve the sandwich with crispy fries on the side?

Ingredients:

- 12 slices of cooked thick-cut bacon
- 1½ lbs. sea scallops, chopped
- 6 soft hamburger buns, split
- 1 teaspoon Tabasco sauce
- ½ cup mayonnaise   • 6 thick tomato slices
- 3 tablespoons ketchup   • Salt and black pepper
- 3 ears of corn, shucked
- 6 lettuce leaves

Directions:

1. Mix scallops with corn, Tabasco sauce, black pepper, ketchup, and mayonnaise in a bowl.
2. Preheat the Breakfast Sandwich Maker until the green PREHEAT light comes on.
3. Lift cover, top rings, and cooking plates.
4. Place half of a bun, cut-side up, inside the bottom tray of the sandwich maker.
5. Arrange a lettuce leaf on top then add ☐ of the scallop mixture, 1 lettuce leaf, a tomato slice, and 2 bacon slices on top.
6. Now lower the cooking plate and top rings. Place the other half of the bun on top. Cover the top hood, and let the sandwich cook for 5 minutes.
7. Rotate the handle of the cooking plate clockwise until it stops.
8. Lift the hood, and the rings and transfer the sandwich to a plate.
9. Repeat the same steps with the remaining ingredients.

Nutritional Value (Amount per Serving):

Calories: 282; Fat: 15g; Sodium: 526mg; Carbs: 20g; Fiber: 0.6g; Sugar: 3.3g; Protein: 16g

Slaw and Cod Sandwiches with Tartar Sauce

Prep Time: 15 Minutes   Cook Time: 15 Minutes   Serves: 4

Preparation and Cooking Tips: Enjoy sautéed veggies on the side for a change of taste.

Serving Suggestion: Serve the sandwich with a cauliflower bacon salad on the side.

Ingredients:

Tartar sauce:
- 1 tablespoon capers, rinsed, drained, and chopped
- 2 teaspoons sweet pickle relish
- 3 tablespoons mayonnaise
- 1 teaspoon Dijon mustard
- 1 teaspoon sugar

Slaw:
- 1 small head of cabbage, shredded
- ½ small red onion, sliced
- 2 teaspoons cider vinegar
- 1 teaspoon Dijon mustard
- 3 tablespoons mayonnaise
- 1 tablespoon sugar

- Salt and black pepper

Fish:
- 12 ounces cod filet, cut into four portions
- 1½ cups all-purpose flour
- 1 teaspoon baking powder
- 4 burger buns, split in half
- 2 quarts peanut oil
- 1 cup light beer
- ½ cup cornstarch
- Salt and black pepper
- ¼ teaspoon paprika

Directions:

1. Mix all the slaw ingredients in a suitable bowl and keep it aside. Whisk all the tartar sauce ingredients in another bowl and set it aside.
2. Mix flour with cornstarch, baking powder, black pepper, salt, paprika, and beer in a bowl.
3. Set a deep frying pan with oil over medium-high heat. Dip the fish in the beer batter, then deep fry until golden brown. Transfer the fried fish to a plate lined with parchment paper.
4. Preheat the Breakfast Sandwich Maker until the green PREHEAT light comes on. Lift cover, top rings, and cooking plates.
5. Place half of a bun, cut-side up, inside the bottom tray of the sandwich maker.
6. Spread ¼ of the fish, slaw, and tartar sauce on top. Now lower the cooking plate and top rings.
7. Place the other half of the bun on top. Cover the top hood, and let the sandwich cook for 5 minutes.
8. Rotate the handle of the cooking plate clockwise until it stops. Lift the hood, and the rings and transfer the sandwich to a plate.
9. Repeat the same with the remaining ingredients.

Nutritional Value (Amount per Serving):

Calories: 391; Fat: 5g; Sodium: 88mg; Carbs: 3g; Fiber: 0g; Sugar: 0g; Protein: 27g

Breadcrumb and Tuna Burgers

Prep Time: 15 Minutes   Cook Time: 11 Minutes   Serves: 4

Preparation and Cooking Tips: Add some additional ground black pepper to the filling.

Serving Suggestion: Serve the sandwich with your favorite sauce on the side.

Ingredients:

- 1 tablespoon celery, chopped
- 2 cups tuna flakes
- ½ cup breadcrumbs

- 1 red onion, minced
- 1 egg, beaten

Sandwich:
- 8 whole wheat bread slices, cut into 4-inch circle
- 4 tablespoons mayonnaise

Directions:

1. Mix the patty ingredients in a bowl. Form into patties.
2. Cook in a pan over medium heat for 2 to 3 minutes per side.
3. Preheat the Breakfast Sandwich Maker until the green PREHEAT light comes on. Lift cover, top rings, and cooking plates.
4. Place one bread slice in the sandwich maker and top it with ¼ mayonnaise.
5. Lower the cooking plate and top rings then add a patty.
6. Add ¼ of the remaining fillings and the other circle of the bread on top. Cover the top hood, and let the sandwich cook for 5 minutes.
7. When finished cooking, rotate the handle of the cooking plate clockwise until it stops.
8. Lift the hood, and the rings and transfer the sandwich to a plate.
9. Repeat the same steps with the remaining ingredients.

Nutritional Value (Amount per Serving):

Calories: 437; Fat: 28g; Sodium: 1221mg; Carbs: 22.3g; Fiber: 0.9g; Sugar: 8g; Protein: 30.3g

Lobster Rolls with Basil

Prep Time: 15 Minutes   Cook Time: 5 Minutes   Serves: 4

Preparation and Cooking Tips: Add a layer of pickled onions for a change of taste.

Serving Suggestion: Would you please serve the sandwich with crispy carrot chips on the side?

Ingredients:

- 1½ lbs. cooked and cubed lobster meat
- 1 pinch salt and black pepper to taste
- 4 large leaf (blank)s lettuce leaves
- 1 tablespoon butter, softened
- 2 medium green onions, chopped
- 4 English muffins, split
- 2 tablespoons mayonnaise
- 1 teaspoon fresh lime juice
- 1 dash of hot pepper sauce

- 1 stalk celery, chopped
- 1 pinch dried basil

Directions:

1. Mix lobster meat with butter, lime juice, hot pepper sauce, green onion, mayonnaise, black pepper, salt, basil, and celery in a bowl.
2. Preheat the Breakfast Sandwich Maker until the green PREHEAT light comes on.
3. Lift cover, top rings, and cooking plates.
4. Place half of the English muffin, cut-side up, inside the bottom tray of the sandwich maker.
5. Arrange a lettuce leaf on top of the English muffin, then add ¼ of the lobster mixture on top.
6. Now lower the cooking plate and top rings. Place the other half of the muffin on top. Cover the top hood, and let the sandwich cook for 5 minutes.
7. Rotate the handle of the cooking plate clockwise until it stops.
8. Lift the hood, and the rings and transfer the sandwich to a plate.
9. Repeat the same steps with the remaining ingredients.

Nutritional Value (Amount per Serving):

Calories: 380; Fat: 20g; Sodium: 686mg; Carbs: 3g; Fiber: 1g; Sugar: 1.2g; Protein: 21g

Thai Cucumber and Tuna Burgers

Prep Time: 15 Minutes   Cook Time: 11 Minutes   Serves: 4

Preparation and Cooking Tips: you can also add a lettuce leaf to the filling.

Serving Suggestion: Would you please serve the sandwich with a broccoli salad on the side?

Ingredients:

- 2 tablespoons chopped dry-roasted peanuts
- 1 Thai or serrano chile, seeded and minced
- 2 Kirby cucumbers, sliced
- ¼ medium red onion, sliced
- 3 tablespoons rice vinegar
- 2 teaspoons fresh ginger, grated
- 1 garlic clove, smashed
- 2 tablespoons Asian fish sauce
- 2 tablespoons cilantro, chopped
- 1 tablespoon basil, chopped
- 1½ lbs. sushi-quality tuna

- 1½ tablespoon vegetable oil
- 1½ teaspoon Asian sesame oil
- 4 hamburger buns, split in half
- 1 teaspoon sugar
- Salt and black pepper

Directions:

1. Blend tuna with basil, fish sauce, serrano chile, garlic, ginger, cilantro, black pepper, sugar, salt, rice vinegar and red onion in a bowl.
2. Make 4 tuna patties out of this mixture and sear them in a pan greased with oil for 3 minutes per side.
3. Preheat the Breakfast Sandwich Maker until the green PREHEAT light comes on.
4. Lift cover, top rings, and cooking plates.
5. Place half of a bun, cut-side up, inside the bottom tray of the sandwich maker.
6. Arrange a seared tuna patty and ¼ of peanuts and cucumbers on top.
7. Now lower the cooking plate and top rings. Place the other half of the bun on top. Cover the top hood, and let the sandwich cook for 5 minutes.
8. Rotate the handle of the cooking plate clockwise until it stops. Lift the hood, and the rings and transfer the sandwich to a plate.
9. Repeat the same steps with the remaining ingredients.

Nutritional Value (Amount per Serving):

Calories: 392; Fat: 16g; Sodium: 466mg; Carbs: 23.9g; Fiber: 0.9g; Sugar: 0.6g; Protein: 48g

Blackened Fish Sandwich

Prep Time: 15 Minutes   Cook Time: 13 Minutes   Serves: 2

Preparation and Cooking Tips: Add some additional dried herbs to the filling.

Serving Suggestion: Serve the sandwich with your favorite sauce on the side.

Ingredients:

- 2 teaspoons blackening seasoning
- 4 whole bread slices, cut into 4-inch circles
- 4 tablespoons mayonnaise
- 1 red onion, sliced thinly • 2 salmon fillets

Directions:

1. Preheat your grill to medium heat. Sprinkle salmon with blackening seasoning. Grill salmon for 4

minutes per side.
2. Preheat the Breakfast Sandwich Maker until the green PREHEAT light comes on.
3. Lift cover, top rings, and cooking plates.
4. Add bread slices inside. Spread with ½ of the mayonnaise.
5. Top with ½ of the grilled salmon and onion slices. Now lower the cooking plate and top rings.
6. Add the other circle of the bread on top. Cover the top hood, and let the sandwich cook for 5 minutes.
7. When finished cooking, rotate the handle of the cooking plate clockwise until it stops.
8. Lift the hood, and the rings and transfer the sandwich to a plate.
9. Repeat the same steps with the remaining ingredients.

Nutritional Value (Amount per Serving):

Calories: 374; Fat: 25g; Sodium: 275mg; Carbs: 7.3g; Fiber: 0g; Sugar: 6g; Protein: 12.3g

Shrimp-Panko Burgers

Prep Time: 15 Minutes   Cook Time: 11 Minutes   Serves: 4

Preparation and Cooking Tips: Add a layer of pickled veggies for a change of taste.

Serving Suggestion: Serve the sandwich with crispy zucchini fries on the side.

Ingredients:

- 1 lb. peeled and deveined large shrimp, chopped
- 1 teaspoon Mexican-style hot sauce
- 4 sesame seed hamburger buns, split
- 1 tablespoon whole-grain mustard
- 1 ripe medium-size avocado, sliced
- 5 tablespoons unsalted butter
- ¾ teaspoon old bay seasoning
- 1½ tablespoons fresh lemon juice
- 1 cup shredded iceberg lettuce
- ½ teaspoon lemon zest   • 1 small tomato, sliced
- ¼ cup scallions, chopped • 1 large egg
- ½ cup mayonnaise   • ¾ cup panko
- 1½ teaspoon salt

Directions:

1. Mix mayonnaise with mustard, hot sauce, salt, old bay seasoning, and scallion in a bowl.
2. Dip the shrimp in the egg then in panko crumbs. Melt butter in a skillet and sear the shrimp for 3

minutes per side until golden brown. Fry all the coated shrimp and transfer them to a plate.

3. Preheat the Breakfast Sandwich Maker until the green PREHEAT light comes on. Lift cover, top rings, and cooking plates.

4. Place half of a bun, cut-side up, inside the bottom tray of the sandwich maker.

5. Arrange a lettuce leaf on top of the bun then add ¼ of the mayonnaise on top.

6. Now lower the cooking plate and top rings, and place ¼ of the shrimp, tomato, avocado, and lettuce on top.

7. Place the other half of the bun on top. Cover the top hood, and let the sandwich cook for 5 minutes.

8. Rotate the handle of the cooking plate clockwise until it stops. Lift the hood, and the rings and transfer the sandwich to a plate.

9. Repeat the same steps with the remaining ingredients.

Nutritional Value (Amount per Serving):

Calories: 305; Fat: 25g; Sodium: 532mg; Carbs: 2.3g; Fiber: 0.4g; Sugar: 2g; Protein: 18.3g

Tartar Cod Sandwich

Prep Time: 15 Minutes   Cook Time: 5 Minutes   Serves: 2

Preparation and Cooking Tips: You can also add a drizzle of paprika on top of the filling.

Serving Suggestion: Serve the sandwich with coleslaw and your favorite sauce on the side.

Ingredients:

- 4 whole wheat bread slices, cut into 4-inch circle
- 2 breaded cod fillets, cooked
- 4 tablespoons tartar sauce
- 4 slices cucumber

Directions:

1. Preheat the Breakfast Sandwich Maker until the green PREHEAT light comes on.

2. Lift cover, top rings, and cooking plates.

3. Place one bread slice in the sandwich maker. Top with ½ of the cucumber and cod fillets.

4. Drizzle with ½ of the tartar sauce. Now lower the cooking plate and top rings.

5. Add the other circle of the bread on top.

6. Cover the top hood, and let the sandwich cook for 5 minutes.

7. When finished cooking, rotate the handle of the cooking plate clockwise until it stops.

8. Lift the hood, and the rings and transfer the sandwich to a plate.

9. Repeat the same steps with the remaining ingredients.

Nutritional Value (Amount per Serving):

Calories: 396; Fat: 23.2g; Sodium: 622mg; Carbs: 0.7g; Fiber: 0g; Sugar: 0g; Protein: 45.6g

Homemade Seafood Burger

Prep Time: 15 Minutes   Cook Time: 11 Minutes   Serves: 4

Preparation and Cooking Tips: you can also add a lettuce leaf to the filling.

Serving Suggestion: Serve the sandwich with crispy sweet potato fries on the side.

Ingredients:

- 2 tablespoons fresh parsley, chopped
- 2 tablespoons dill, chopped
- ½ lb. skinless halibut
- 2 green onions, chopped
- 1 tablespoon lemon zest
- Juice from half a lemon
- ½ lb. prawns
- ½ lb. scallops
- ½ cup panko breadcrumbs
- 3 tablespoons neutral oil
- 4 burger buns, cut in half
- 3 tablespoons butter
- ½ red chilli
- 3 eggs
- Salt and black pepper

Directions:

1. Blend prawns, halibut, green onions, parsley, lemon zest, lemon juice, scallops, dill, red chili, salt, and black pepper in a food processor. Make 4 patties out of this seafood mixture.

2. Beat eggs with black pepper and salt then dip patties in them.

3. Coat the patties with the panko breadcrumbs. Set a pan with oil and butter on medium-high heat. Sear the patties in the hot oil for 3 minutes per side.

4. Preheat the Breakfast Sandwich Maker until the green PREHEAT light comes on. Lift cover, top rings, and cooking plates.

5. Place half of a bun, cut-side up, inside the bottom tray of the sandwich maker.

6. Place a seafood patty on top. Now lower the cooking

plate and top rings.

7. Place the other half of the muffin on top. Cover the top hood, and let the sandwich cook for 5 minutes.
8. Rotate the handle of the cooking plate clockwise until it stops. Lift the hood, and the rings and transfer the sandwich to a plate.
9. Repeat the same steps with the remaining ingredients.

Nutritional Value (Amount per Serving):

Calories: 425; Fat: 15g; Sodium: 345mg; Carbs: 2.3g; Fiber: 1.4g; Sugar: 3g; Protein: 23.3g

Crab Melt and Mushrooms Sandwich

Prep Time: 15 Minutes   Cook Time: 5 Minutes   Serves: 4

Preparation and Cooking Tips: Add a layer of pickled onions for a change of taste.
Serving Suggestion: Serve the sandwich with crispy bacon and your favorite keto sauce on the side.

Ingredients:

- 4 large Portobello mushrooms cap, split in half
- ½ cup finely shredded cheddar cheese
- ½ teaspoon Worcestershire sauce
- ½ teaspoon old bay seasoning
- 1 tablespoon chopped parsley
- 8 ounces of lump crab meat
- 3 tablespoons mayonnaise
- ¼ teaspoon sea salt
- Dash black pepper
- Dash cayenne pepper
- 4 green onions sliced
- Spray coconut oil
- Salt and pepper

Directions:

1. Mix crab meat with mayonnaise, old bay seasoning, Worcestershire sauce, cayenne pepper, black pepper, salt, parsley, and onion.
2. Preheat the Breakfast Sandwich Maker until the green PREHEAT light comes on.
3. Lift cover, top rings, and cooking plates.
4. Place one circle of the mushroom in the sandwich maker.
5. Top it with cheese and ¼ of the crab mixture. Now lower the cooking plate and top rings.
6. Add the other circle of the mushroom on top. Cover the top hood, and let the sandwich cook for 5 minutes.
7. Rotate the handle of the cooking plate clockwise

until it stops.

8. Lift the hood, and the rings and transfer the sandwich to a plate.
9. Repeat the same with the remaining ingredients.

Nutritional Value (Amount per Serving):

Calories: 395; Fat: 9.5g; Sodium: 655mg; Carbs: 3.4g; Fiber: 0.4g; Sugar: 0.4g; Protein: 28.3g

Lemony Shrimp and Cod Burgers

Prep Time: 15 Minutes   Cook Time: 15 Minutes   Serves: 4

Preparation and Cooking Tips: Add a layer of spicy mayo and pickled veggies for a change of taste.
Serving Suggestion: Would you please serve the sandwich with crispy fries on the side?

Ingredients:

- 12 ounces medium shrimp, peeled, deveined, and cut into chunks
- 8 ounces cod, cut into chunks
- ¾ cup fresh breadcrumbs
- ¼ cup drained capers, rinsed
- 2 medium scallions, sliced
- 3 tablespoons chopped parsley
- ¾ teaspoon black pepper
- Vegetable oil, for brushing
- 4 hamburger buns, split in half
- ¼ cup lemon juice
- 1¼ teaspoon salt

Directions:

1. Blend shrimp, capers, scallions, parsley, crumbs, lemon juice, cod, black pepper, and salt in a food processor for 1 minute.
2. Make 4 patties out of this mixture and sear them in a skillet greased with oil for 5 minutes per side.
3. Preheat the Breakfast Sandwich Maker until the green PREHEAT light comes on.
4. Lift cover, top rings, and cooking plates.
5. Place half of a bun, cut-side up, inside the bottom tray of the sandwich maker. Now lower the cooking plate and top rings.
6. Place a patty, a lettuce leaf, and the other top half of the bun on top. Cover the top hood, and let the burger cook for 5 minutes.
7. Rotate the handle of the cooking plate clockwise until it stops.
8. Lift the hood, and the rings and transfer the burger

to a plate.

9. Repeat the same steps with the remaining ingredients.

Nutritional Value (Amount per Serving):

Calories: 325; Fat: 16g; Sodium: 431mg; Carbs: 2g; Fiber: 1.2g; Sugar: 4g; Protein: 23g

Mayo Tuna Cheese Sandwich

Prep Time: 15 Minutes   Cook Time: 5 Minutes   Serves: 2

Preparation and Cooking Tips: Add some additional ground black pepper to the filling.

Serving Suggestion: Serve the sandwich with crispy bacon and your favorite sauce on the side.

Ingredients:

- 1 tablespoon green onion, minced
- 2 mozzarella Cheese, slices
- 4 tablespoons mayonnaise
- 1 tablespoon celery, minced
- 1 cup tuna flakes   • 2 burger buns, split

Directions:

1. Mix all ingredients except buns and cheese.
2. Preheat the Breakfast Sandwich Maker until the green PREHEAT light comes on.
3. Lift cover, top rings, and cooking plates. Add one burger bun inside.
4. Spread with ½ of the tuna mixture. Top with ½ of the cheese.
5. Now lower the cooking plate and top rings.
6. Place the other half of the bun on top. Cover the top hood, and let the sandwich cook for 5 minutes.
7. When finished cooking, rotate the handle of the cooking plate clockwise until it stops.
8. Lift the hood, and the rings and transfer the sandwich to a plate.
9. Repeat the same steps with the remaining ingredients.

Nutritional Value (Amount per Serving):

Calories: 459; Fat: 17.7g; Sodium: 1516mg; Carbs: 1.7g; Fiber: 0.5g; Sugar: 0.4g; Protein: 69.2g

Lemony Carrot and Salmon Sandwich

Prep Time: 15 Minutes   Cook Time: 5 Minutes   Serves: 2

Preparation and Cooking Tips: You can also add lettuce leaves to the filling.

Serving Suggestion: Serve the sandwich with coleslaw and your favorite sauce on the side.

Ingredients:

- 2 tablespoons carrot, shredded
- 2 tablespoons celery, minced
- 2 burger buns, split in half
- 1 tablespoon mayonnaise
- 1 tablespoon lemon juice
- 1 cup salmon flakes
- ¼ cup cream cheese
- 1 teaspoon dill weed
- Salt and black pepper

Directions:

1. Combine all the ingredients except burger buns.
2. Preheat the Breakfast Sandwich Maker until the green PREHEAT light comes on.
3. Lift cover, top rings, and cooking plates.
4. Add burger bottoms inside. Spread with ½ of the salmon mixture.
5. Now lower the cooking plate and top rings. Place the other half of the bun on top.
6. Cover the top hood, and let the sandwich cook for 5 minutes.
7. When finished cooking, rotate the handle of the cooking plate clockwise until it stops.
8. Lift the hood, and the rings and transfer the sandwich to a plate.
9. Repeat the same steps with the remaining ingredients.

Nutritional Value (Amount per Serving):

Calories: 310; Fat: 17g; Sodium: 271mg; Carbs: 4.3g; Fiber: 0.9g; Sugar: 2.1g; Protein: 35g

Olives and Tuna Burgers

Prep Time: 15 Minutes   Cook Time: 5 Minutes   Serves: 4

Preparation and Cooking Tips: Add a layer of spicy mayo and pickled veggies for a change of taste.

Serving Suggestion: Would you please serve the sandwich with crispy carrot chips on the side?

Ingredients:

- 12 pitted Kalamata olives, coarsely chopped
- 1 tablespoon salted capers, rinsed and minced
- 1½ teaspoon anchovy paste

- 1¼ lbs. fresh tuna, diced
- 2 scallions, sliced
- Salt and black pepper
- Olive oil, for brushing
- ¼ cup mayonnaise
- 4 brioche buns, split

Directions:

1. Mix tuna meat with scallions, olives, and capers in a bowl.
2. Preheat the Breakfast Sandwich Maker until the green PREHEAT light comes on.
3. Lift cover, top rings, and cooking plates.
4. Place half of a bun, cut-side up, inside the bottom tray of the sandwich maker.
5. Add ¼ of mayo, anchovy paste, and tuna mixture on top.
6. Place the other half of the bun on top. Lower the top plate and ring. Cover the top hood, and let the sandwich cook for 5 minutes.
7. Rotate the handle of the cooking plate clockwise until it stops.
8. Lift the hood, and the rings and transfer the sandwich to a plate.
9. Repeat the same steps with the remaining ingredients.

Nutritional Value (Amount per Serving):

Calories: 309; Fat: 25g; Sodium: 463mg; Carbs: 19.9g; Fiber: 0.3g; Sugar: 0.3g; Protein: 18g

Mayo Shrimp Sandwich

Prep Time: 15 Minutes   Cook Time: 5 Minutes   Serves: 4

Preparation and Cooking Tips: Add some additional dried herbs to the filling.

Serving Suggestion: Serve the sandwich with your favorite sauce on the side.

Ingredients:

- 1 cup shrimp, cooked, peeled, deveined and chopped
- 4 tablespoons mayonnaise
- 1 teaspoon lemon juice
- 1 teaspoon dried dill
- 4 burger buns

Directions:

1. Combine all ingredients except buns.
2. Preheat the Breakfast Sandwich Maker until the

green PREHEAT light comes on.
3. Lift cover, top rings, and cooking plates.
4. Place the lower half of the bun in the sandwich maker and top it with ¼ th of the shrimp mixture.
5. Now lower the cooking plate and top rings. Place the other half of the bun on top.
6. Cover the top hood, and let the sandwich cook for 5 minutes.
7. When finished cooking, rotate the handle of the cooking plate clockwise until it stops.
8. Lift the hood, and the rings and transfer the sandwich to a plate.
9. Repeat the same steps with the remaining ingredients.

Nutritional Value (Amount per Serving):

Calories: 330; Fat: 10.4g; Sodium: 690 mg; Carbs: 11.4g; Fiber: 3g; Sugar: 4.7g; Protein: 48 g

Salsa Cod Sandwich

Prep Time: 15 Minutes   Cook Time: 5 Minutes   Serves: 2

Preparation and Cooking Tips: Add some additional dried herbs to the filling.

Serving Suggestion: Serve the sandwich with crispy bacon and your favorite sauce on the side.

Ingredients:

- 4 whole wheat bread slices, cut into 4-inch circle
- 2 cod fillets, grilled and sliced into strips
- 1 teaspoon sweet pickle relish
- ½ teaspoon dried parsley flakes
- 4 tablespoons salsa

Directions:

1. Preheat the Breakfast Sandwich Maker until the green PREHEAT light comes on.
2. Lift cover, top rings, and cooking plates.
3. Place one bread slice in the sandwich maker.
4. Top with ½ of the cod fillets, salsa, and sweet pickle relish.
5. Sprinkle with parsley flakes. Now lower the cooking plate and top rings.
6. Add the other circle of the bread on top. Cover the top hood, and let the sandwich cook for 5 minutes.
7. When finished cooking, rotate the handle of the cooking plate clockwise until it stops.
8. Lift the hood, and the rings and transfer the sandwich to a plate.

9. Repeat the same steps with the remaining ingredients.

Nutritional Value (Amount per Serving):

Calories: 410; Fat: 17.8g; Sodium: 619mg; Carbs: 21g; Fiber: 1.4g; Sugar: 1.8g; Protein: 38.4g

Mexican-style Seafood Burger

Prep Time: 15 Minutes   Cook Time: 15 Minutes   Serves: 4

Preparation and Cooking Tips: Add a layer of sliced bell peppers for a change of taste.

Serving Suggestion: Serve the sandwich with a cauliflower bacon salad on the side.

Ingredients:

- 8 ounces hill country fare chipotle mayo
- 1 crunch chopped salad kit
- 4 English muffins, split in half
- 4 salmon patties

Directions:

1. Sear the salmon patties in a skillet for 5 minutes per side.
2. Preheat the Breakfast Sandwich Maker until the green PREHEAT light comes on.
3. Lift cover, top rings, and cooking plates.
4. Place half of a muffin, cut-side up, inside the bottom tray of the sandwich maker.
5. Spread ¼ mayonnaise, a salmon patty, and ¼ chopped salad on top.
6. Now lower the cooking plate and top rings. Place the other half of the muffin on top. Cover the top hood, and let the burger cook for 5 minutes.
7. Rotate the handle of the cooking plate clockwise until it stops.
8. Lift the hood, and the rings and transfer the burger to a plate.
9. Repeat the same steps with the remaining ingredients.

Nutritional Value (Amount per Serving):

Calories: 361; Fat: 16g; Sodium: 515mg; Carbs: 29.3g; Fiber: 0.1g; Sugar: 18.2g; Protein: 33.3g

Chapter 6: Normal Sandwiches and Omelets

Sausage Muffin Sandwich

Prep Time: 15 Minutes   Cook Time: 5 Minutes   Serves: 1

Preparation and Cooking Tips: Add a layer of sliced bell peppers for a change of taste.

Serving Suggestion: Would you please serve the sandwich with crispy carrot chips on the side?

Ingredients:

- 1 breakfast sausage patty, cooked
- 1 handful of fresh chives, chopped
- Hot sauce and honey, for serving
- 1 tablespoon unsalted butter
- 1 English muffin, split
- 2 slices American cheese
- 2 large eggs, beaten
- Salt and black pepper

Directions:

1. Beat eggs with black pepper, chives, honey, salt, and hot sauce in a bowl.
2. Preheat the Breakfast Sandwich Maker until the green PREHEAT light comes on.
3. Lift cover, top rings, and cooking plates.
4. Place half of the English muffin, cut-side up, inside the bottom tray of the sandwich maker. Brush it with butter. Add sausage patty on top.
5. Now lower the cooking plate and top rings, then pour in the egg.
6. Place a cheese slice and the other half of the muffin on top.
7. Cover the top hood, and let the sandwich cook for 5 minutes.
8. Rotate the handle of the cooking plate clockwise until it stops.
9. Lift the hood, and the rings and transfer the sandwich to a plate.

Nutritional Value (Amount per Serving):

Calories: 375; Fat: 16g; Sodium: 255mg; Carbs: 4.1g; Fiber: 1.2g; Sugar: 5g; Protein: 24.1g

Mexican Fried Egg Sandwich

Prep Time: 15 Minutes   Cook Time: 15 Minutes   Serves: 1

Preparation and Cooking Tips: you can also add a lettuce leaf to the filling.

Serving Suggestion: Serve the sandwich with crispy bacon and your favorite sauce on the side.

Ingredients:

Sandwich:

- ½ teaspoon chilli powder
- Fresh cilantro, for garnish
- ¼ cup refried beans
- 2 teaspoons olive oil
- 1 hamburger bun, split
- ¼ sliced avocado
- 2 slices of crispy bacon
- Hot sauce, for garnish
- 1 fried egg

Mexican-style simple syrup:

- ¾ cup Piloncillo sugar
- ½ cup water
- ½ cup whole cloves
- 1 raw almond, chopped
- Peel 1 orange
- 4 cinnamon sticks

Directions:

1. Add sugar, whole cloves, orange peel, water, cinnamon sticks, and almonds to a saucepan. Cook for 10 minutes on low heat, then strain.
2. Preheat the Breakfast Sandwich Maker until the green PREHEAT light comes on.
3. Lift cover, top rings, and cooking plates.
4. Place half of the English muffin, cut-side up, inside the bottom tray of the sandwich maker.
5. Spread the prepared syrup, refried beans, and the rest of the ingredients on top.
6. Now lower the cooking plate and top rings. Place the other half of the muffin on top.
7. Cover the top hood, and let the sandwich cook for 5 minutes.
8. Rotate the handle of the cooking plate clockwise until it stops.
9. Lift the hood, and the rings and transfer the sandwich to a plate.

Nutritional Value (Amount per Serving):

Calories: 373; Fat: 8g; Sodium: 146mg; Carbs: 8g; Fiber: 5g; Sugar: 1g; Protein: 23g

Cheese and Spinach Sandwiches

Prep Time: 15 Minutes   Cook Time: 5 Minutes   Serves: 2

Preparation and Cooking Tips: You can also add a layer of your favorite sauce to the filling.

Serving Suggestion: Serve the sandwich with your favorite sauce on the side.

Ingredients:

- 1 tablespoon snipped fresh rosemary
- 2 cups fresh baby spinach leaves
- 1 tomato, cut into 8 thin slices
- 4 tablespoons low-fat feta cheese
- Freshly ground black pepper.
- 4 teaspoons olive oil
- ⅛ teaspoon kosher salt
- 2 buns, sliced
- 4 eggs, beaten

Directions:

1. Beat eggs with black pepper and salt in a suitable bowl.
2. Preheat the Breakfast Sandwich Maker until the green PREHEAT light comes on.
3. Lift cover, top rings, and cooking plates. Place the lower half of a bun in the sandwich maker.
4. Top it with half of the toppings except the egg mixture.
5. Now lower the cooking plate and top rings, then pour in half of the egg.
6. Place the other half of the bun on top. Cover the top hood, and let the sandwich cook for 5 minutes.
7. When finished cooking, rotate the handle of the cooking plate clockwise until it stops.
8. Lift the hood, and the rings and transfer the sandwich to a plate.
9. Repeat the same with the remaining ingredients.

Nutritional Value (Amount per Serving):

Calories: 237; Fat: 19g; Sodium: 518mg; Carbs: 7g; Fiber: 1.5g; Sugar: 3.4g; Protein: 12g

Classic Lettuce, Bacon, and Tomato Sandwich

Prep Time: 15 Minutes   Cook Time: 5 Minutes   Serves: 1

Preparation and Cooking Tips: Add some additional ground black pepper to the filling.

Serving Suggestion: Serve the sandwich with crispy bacon and your favorite sauce on the side.

Ingredients:

- 2 slices white bread, cut in a 4-inch circle
- 1 leaf Romaine lettuce, torn in half
- 3 bacon slices, cooked
- 2 thin tomato slices
- 2 teaspoons mayonnaise

Directions:

1. Preheat the Breakfast Sandwich Maker until the green PREHEAT light comes on.
2. Lift cover, top rings, and cooking plates.
3. Place one-half of the bread in the sandwich maker.
4. Top it with mayonnaise, lettuce and tomato.
5. Lower the cooking plate and top rings, then place the bacon on top.
6. Place the other half of the bread on top. Add the other circle of the bread on top.
7. Cover the top hood, and let the sandwich cook for 5 minutes.
8. When finished cooking, rotate the handle of the cooking plate clockwise until it stops.
9. Lift the hood, and the rings and transfer the sandwich to a plate.

Nutritional Value (Amount per Serving):

Calories: 267; Fat: 12g; Sodium: 165mg; Carbs: 39g; Fiber: 1.4g; Sugar: 22g; Protein: 3.3g

Fried Honey-butter Chicken Biscuits

Prep Time: 15 Minutes   Cook Time: 15 Minutes   Serves: 4

Preparation and Cooking Tips: you can also add a lettuce leaf to the filling.

Serving Suggestion: Serve the sandwich with a cauliflower bacon salad on the side.

Ingredients:

Honey butter:
- ½ cup unsalted butter
- ½ teaspoon kosher salt
- ¼ cup honey

Chicken cutlets:
- ¼ teaspoon cayenne pepper
- ¼ teaspoon black pepper
- 4 boneless chicken cutlets
- 1 tablespoon hot sauce
- 1 cup buttermilk
- ½ teaspoon salt

For cooking:
- 2 cups Japanese breadcrumbs
- Vegetable oil, for frying
- Black pepper, to taste
- 4 pies-n-thighs biscuits

- Hot sauce, for serving

Directions:

1. Mix chicken cutlets with buttermilk, black pepper, cayenne pepper, salt, and hot sauce in a suitable bowl. Cover and marinate this chicken for 30 minutes at least in the refrigerator.
2. Meanwhile, mix butter with salt and honey in a bowl. Remove the chicken from its marinade, and coat it with a honey mixture. Coat the honey chicken with panko crumbs and drizzle black pepper on top.
3. Set a pan with vegetable oil for frying on medium-high heat. Fry the chicken cutlets until golden brown and keep them aside.
4. Preheat the Breakfast Sandwich Maker until the green PREHEAT light comes on. Lift cover, top rings, and cooking plates.
5. Place half a biscuit, cut-side up, inside the bottom tray of the sandwich maker.
6. Now lower the cooking plate and top rings, then place a chicken cutlet and add breadcrumbs.
7. Place the other half of the muffin on top. Cover the top hood, and let it cook for 5 minutes.
8. Rotate the handle of the cooking plate clockwise until it stops. Lift the hood, and the rings and transfer the biscuit to a plate.
9. Repeat the same steps with the remaining ingredients.

Nutritional Value (Amount per Serving):

Calories: 380; Fat: 19g; Sodium: 318mg; Carbs: 9g; Fiber: 5g; Sugar: 3g; Protein: 26g

Egg, Parmesan, and Spinach Sandwich

Prep Time: 15 Minutes   Cook Time: 5 Minutes   Serves: 1

Preparation and Cooking Tips: You can also add lettuce leaves to the filling.

Serving Suggestion: Serve the sandwich with crispy bacon and your favorite sauce on the side.

Ingredients:

- 1 tablespoon grated parmesan cheese
- 1 toasted English muffin, sliced
- ½ cup baby spinach leaves
- 2 large egg whites
- 1 garlic clove, minced

Directions:

1. Preheat the Breakfast Sandwich Maker until the green PREHEAT light comes on.
2. Lift cover, top rings, and cooking plates.
3. Place half of the English muffin, cut-side up, inside the bottom tray of the sandwich maker.
4. Arrange the baby spinach leaves on top of the English muffin.
5. Beat the egg whites, parmesan cheese, and garlic in a small bowl.
6. Lower the cooking plate and top rings then pour in the egg mixture.
7. Place the other half of the muffin on top. Cover the top hood, and let the sandwich cook for 5 minutes.
8. When finished cooking, rotate the handle of the cooking plate clockwise until it stops.
9. Lift the hood, and the rings and transfer the sandwich to a plate.

Nutritional Value (Amount per Serving):

Calories: 282; Fat: 15g; Sodium: 526mg; Carbs: 20g; Fiber: 0.6g; Sugar: 3.3g; Protein: 16g

Frittata Sandwich with Olive Salad

Prep Time: 15 Minutes   Cook Time: 10 Minutes   Serves: 4

Preparation and Cooking Tips: Add a layer of pickled onions for a change of taste.

Serving Suggestion: Serve the sandwich with crispy sweet potato fries on the side.

Ingredients:

- ½ teaspoons crushed red pepper flakes
- ½ cup fresh parsley leaves, chopped
- 2 tablespoons red onion, chopped
- 8 bread slices, cut into 4 inches round
- 2 tablespoons red wine vinegar
- ¾ cup green olives, chopped
- 2 tablespoons capers
- ¼ cup olive oil
- ½ teaspoon sugar
- 8 eggs
- 4 cups kale leaves
- Salt and black pepper

Directions:

1. Sauté red onion with red pepper flakes, capers,

black pepper, sugar, oil, salt, and vinegar in a skillet for 5 minutes.

2. Preheat the Breakfast Sandwich Maker until the green PREHEAT light comes on.
3. Lift cover, top rings, and cooking plates. Place one bread slice inside the bottom tray of the sandwich maker.
4. Beat the eggs with onion mixture, black pepper, and salt in a small bowl.
5. Lower the cooking plate and top rings then pour in ⅛ of the egg mixture.
6. Place another bread slice on top. Cover the top hood, and let the sandwich cook for 5 minutes.
7. Rotate the handle of the cooking plate clockwise until it stops.
8. Lift the hood, and the rings and transfer the sandwich to a plate.
9. Repeat the same steps with the remaining ingredients.

Nutritional Value (Amount per Serving):

Calories: 322; Fat: 12g; Sodium: 202mg; Carbs: 24.6g; Fiber: 4g; Sugar: 8g; Protein: 17.3g

Avocado, and Cucumber Sandwich

Prep Time: 15 Minutes   Cook Time: 5 Minutes   Serves: 2

Preparation and Cooking Tips: you can also add lettuce leaves to the filling.

Serving Suggestion: Serve the sandwich with crispy zucchini fries on the side.

Ingredients:

- 4 slices grainy bread, cut into 4 inches round
- ½ head of butter lettuce, leaves torn
- ¼ English cucumber, sliced
- 8 ounces mozzarella, sliced
- ¼ cup chives, chopped
- ¼ cup mayonnaise
- ¼ cup tarragon
- ¼ cup Greek yogurt
- 1 lemon, halved
- 2 tablespoons olive oil
- 1 avocado, sliced
- 2 cups alfalfa sprouts
- Salt and black pepper

Directions:

1. Beat yogurt with tarragon, chives, mayonnaise, black pepper, and salt.
2. Preheat the Breakfast Sandwich Maker until the green PREHEAT light comes on.

3. Lift cover, top rings, and cooking plates.
4. Place one bread slice inside the bottom tray of the sandwich maker.
5. Add ¼ lettuce, cucumber, avocado, and the rest of the fillings.
6. Now lower the cooking plate and top rings. Place another bread slice on top, then brush it with oil. Cover the top hood, and let the sandwich cook for 5 minutes.
7. Rotate the handle of the cooking plate clockwise until it stops.
8. Lift the hood, and the rings and transfer the sandwich to a plate.
9. Repeat the same steps with the remaining ingredients.

Nutritional Value (Amount per Serving):

Calories: 284; Fat: 7.9g; Sodium: 704mg; Carbs: 6g; Fiber: 3.6g; Sugar: 6g; Protein: 18g

Waffle and Sausage Sandwich with Maple Syrup

Prep Time: 15 Minutes   Cook Time: 5 Minutes   Serves: 1

Serving Suggestion: Serve the sandwich with your favorite sauce on the side.

Preparation and Cooking Tips: You can also add lettuce leaves to the filling.

Ingredients:

- 1 pork sausage patty, cooked
- 2 round frozen waffles
- 1 large egg, beaten
- 1 teaspoon maple syrup

Directions:

1. Preheat the Breakfast Sandwich Maker until the green PREHEAT light comes on.
2. Lift cover, top rings, and cooking plates.
3. Place one of the waffles in the sandwich maker and top it with a patty.
4. Now lower the cooking plate and top rings, then crack the egg onto the cooking plate and drizzle maple syrup on top.
5. Place the other top half of the waffle on top.
6. Cover the top hood, and let the sandwich cook for 5 minutes.
7. When finished cooking, rotate the handle of the cooking plate clockwise until it stops.

8. Lift the hood, and the rings and transfer the sandwich to a plate.

Nutritional Value (Amount per Serving):

Calories: 284; Fat: 7.9g; Sodium: 704mg; Carbs: 38.1g; Fiber: 1.9g; Sugar: 1.9g; Protein: 14.8g

Maple Sausage and Cheddar Biscuit Sandwich

Prep Time: 15 Minutes   Cook Time: 5 Minutes   Serves: 1

Preparation and Cooking Tips: Add some additional dried herbs to the filling.

Serving Suggestion: Serve the sandwich with your favorite sauce on the side.

Ingredients:

- 1 maple pork sausage patty, cooked
- 1 buttermilk biscuit, sliced
- 1 slice of cheddar cheese
- 1 large egg, beaten

Directions:

1. Preheat the Breakfast Sandwich Maker until the green PREHEAT light comes on.
2. Lift cover, top rings, and cooking plates.
3. Place half of the biscuit, cut-side up, inside the bottom tray of the sandwich maker.
4. Arrange the sausage patty on top of the biscuit and top with a slice of cheddar cheese.
5. Slide the egg tray into place and pour the beaten egg into it.
6. Top the egg with the other top half of the biscuit.
7. Cover the top hood, and let the sandwich cook for 5 minutes.
8. When finished cooking, rotate the handle of the cooking plate clockwise until it stops.
9. Lift the hood, and the rings and transfer the sandwich to a plate.

Nutritional Value (Amount per Serving):

Calories: 270; Fat: 14.6g; Sodium: 394mg; Carbs: 31.3g; Fiber: 7.5g; Sugar: 9.7g; Protein: 6.4g

Hearty Forager Sandwich

Prep Time: 15 Minutes   Cook Time: 15 Minutes   Serves: 4

Preparation and Cooking Tips: Add a layer of spicy mayo and pickled veggies for a change of taste.

Serving Suggestion: Would you please serve the sandwich with a broccoli salad on the side?

Ingredients:

Sautéed kale:

- ½ teaspoon crushed red pepper flakes
- 2 large bunches of kale, chopped
- 2 tablespoons olive oil
- 1 medium onion, chopped
- 2 garlic cloves, chopped
- Salt and black pepper

Marinated mushrooms:

- 4 ounces King trumpet mushrooms, sliced
- ¼ cup white wine vinegar
- 1½ teaspoons kosher salt
- ½ shallot, sliced
- 1 sprig thyme
- ¼ cup olive oil

Mushroom mayonnaise:

- 1 tablespoon fresh lemon juice
- 1 teaspoon rosemary, chopped
- ¼ cup dried mushrooms
- ½ shallot, chopped
- ½ cup mayonnaise
- Salt and black pepper

Assembly:

- 4 teaspoons green chile hot sauce
- 1 tablespoon unsalted butter
- 2 tablespoons olive oil
- 4 English muffins, split
- 4 slices Swiss cheese
- 4 large eggs

Directions:

1. Mix all the marinated mushroom ingredients in a bowl, cover, and refrigerate for 1 hour at least. Sauté the marinated mushrooms in a skillet for 5 minutes, then keep them aside.
2. Add all the sautéed kale ingredients to a skillet and cook for 3 minutes, then transfer to a plate.
3. Soak dried mushrooms in water in a bowl for 10 minutes, then drain and chop. Mix the rehydrated mushrooms with the rest of the mushroom mayonnaise ingredients in a bowl.
4. Preheat the Breakfast Sandwich Maker until the green PREHEAT light comes on. Lift cover, top rings, and cooking plates.
5. Place half of the English muffin, cut-side up, inside

the bottom tray of the sandwich maker. Spread ¼ of the mushroom mayonnaise, marinated mushrooms, and kale on top.

6. Beat the eggs in a small bowl. Now lower the cooking plate and top rings, then pour in the egg.
7. Place a cheese slice and another top half of the muffin on top, then brush it with butter. Cover the top hood, and let the sandwich cook for 5 minutes.
8. Rotate the handle of the cooking plate clockwise until it stops. Lift the hood, and the rings and transfer the sandwich to a plate.
9. Repeat the same steps with the remaining muffins and ingredients.

Nutritional Value (Amount per Serving):

Calories: 297; Fat: 15g; Sodium: 548mg; Carbs: 5g; Fiber: 4g; Sugar: 1g; Protein: 19g

Creamy Scrambled Egg Sandwich

Prep Time: 15 Minutes   Cook Time: 5 Minutes   Serves: 2

Preparation and Cooking Tips: Add a layer of spicy mayo and pickled veggies for a change of taste.
Serving Suggestion: Would you please serve the sandwich with a broccoli salad on the side?

Ingredients:

- 4 thick potato bread slices, cut into 4 inches round
- 1 small pinch of cayenne pepper
- 2 tablespoons unsalted butter
- 3 tablespoons cream cheese
- Kosher salt, to taste
- 4 American cheese slices
- Scrambled eggs
- 4 large eggs

Directions:

1. Beat egg with butter, cream cheese, cayenne pepper, and salt in a bowl.
2. Preheat the Breakfast Sandwich Maker until the green PREHEAT light comes on.
3. Lift cover, top rings, and cooking plates.
4. Place one bread slice, inside the bottom tray of the sandwich maker.
5. Lower the cooking plate and top rings, then pour in ¼ the egg.
6. Place one cheese slice and the other bread slice on top. Cover the top hood, and let the sandwich cook

for 5 minutes.
7. Rotate the handle of the cooking plate clockwise until it stops.
8. Lift the hood, and the rings and transfer the sandwich to a plate.
9. Repeat the same steps with the remaining ingredients.

Nutritional Value (Amount per Serving):

Calories: 348; Fat: 12g; Sodium: 710mg; Carbs: 4g; Fiber: 5g; Sugar: 3g; Protein: 31g

Egg Sandwich with Bacon

Prep Time: 15 Minutes   Cook Time: 15 Minutes   Serves: 2

Preparation and Cooking Tips: Enjoy sautéed veggies on the side for a change of taste.
Serving Suggestion: Serve the sandwich with a cauliflower bacon salad on the side.

Ingredients:

- 4 (¾-inch-thick) sourdough bread slices, cut into 4-inch round
- 4 teaspoons Hot sauce, for serving
- 2 tablespoons unsalted butter
- 4 slices thick-cut bacon
- 4 large eggs
- 4 slices cheddar
- Salt and black pepper

Directions:

1. Sauté bacon in a skillet for 5 minutes per side until golden brown.
2. Preheat the Breakfast Sandwich Maker until the green PREHEAT light comes on.
3. Lift cover, top rings, and cooking plates. Place a bread slice, inside the bottom tray of the sandwich maker. Spread the butter on top of the bread.
4. Arrange 2 bacon slices on top of the English muffin.
5. Beat the egg with black pepper and salt in a small bowl.
6. Now lower the cooking plate and top rings, then pour in the egg.
7. Place a cheddar cheese slice and the other bread slice on top. Cover the top hood, and let the sandwich cook for 5 minutes.
8. Rotate the handle of the cooking plate clockwise until it stops. Lift the hood, and the rings and transfer the sandwich to a plate.

9. Repeat the same step with the remaining ingredients.

Nutritional Value (Amount per Serving):

Calories: 311; Fat: 12.5g; Sodium: 595mg; Carbs: 3g; Fiber: 12g; Sugar: 12g; Protein: 17g

Beef Hamburger with Ketchup

Prep Time: 15 Minutes   Cook Time: 7 Minutes   Serves: 2

Preparation and Cooking Tips: Add some additional dried herbs to the filling.

Serving Suggestion: Serve the sandwich with coleslaw and your favorite sauce on the side.

Ingredients:

Hamburger:
- 4 soft hamburger buns, split in half
- Ketchup, mustard, relish, sliced pickles
- Lettuce, tomato slices

Hamburger Pattie:
- 2-pound minced beef
- 3 onions, sliced into rings
- 2 tablespoons oil
- 4 slices cheese
- Salt and black pepper

Directions:

1. Separate beef into 4 equal portions. Form patties the size of your buns. Season generously with salt and black pepper on both sides. Make a dent on one side.
2. Heat 1 tablespoon oil in a skillet over high heat. Add onion and cook until wilted and caramelized. Season with salt and pepper, and then remove.
3. Heat 1 tablespoon oil in a suitable pan until smoking. Add patties and cook for almost 2 minutes until deep golden with a great crust.
4. Preheat the Breakfast Sandwich Maker until the green PREHEAT light comes on.
5. Lift cover, top rings, and cooking plates. Place the lower half of a bun in the sandwich maker.
6. Top it with ¼ ketchup, mustard, pickles, and tomato slices. Now lower the cooking plate and top rings then place a patty on top.
7. Place the other half of the bun on top. Cover the top hood, and let the sandwich cook for 5 minutes.
8. When finished cooking, rotate the handle of the cooking plate clockwise until it stops. Lift the hood,

and the rings and transfer the sandwich to a plate.
9. Repeat the same with the remaining ingredients.

Nutritional Value (Amount per Serving):

Calories: 229; Fat: 1.9; Sodium: 567mg; Carbs: 1.9g; Fiber: 0.4g; Sugar: 0.6g; Protein: 11.8g

Cheese and Egg Sandwich

Prep Time: 15 Minutes   Cook Time: 5 Minutes   Serves: 1

Preparation and Cooking Tips: Add some additional dried herbs to the filling.

Serving Suggestion: Serve the sandwich with coleslaw and your favorite sauce on the side.

Ingredients:

- 1 large egg, beaten
- Butter, or olive oil
- 1 English Muffin
- 1 cheese slice

Directions:

1. Preheat the Breakfast Sandwich Maker until the green PREHEAT light comes on.
2. Lift cover, top rings, and cooking plates.
3. Place the lower half of the muffin in the sandwich maker.
4. Brush the top of the muffin half with butter.
5. Lower the cooking plate and top rings then pour in the egg.
6. Top the egg with a cheese slice and place the other half of the muffin on top.
7. Cover the top hood, and let the sandwich cook for 5 minutes.
8. When finished cooking, rotate the handle of the cooking plate clockwise until it stops.
9. Lift the hood, and the rings and transfer the sandwich to a plate.

Nutritional Value (Amount per Serving):

Calories: 273; Fat: 22g; Sodium: 517mg; Carbs: 3.3g; Fiber: 0.2g; Sugar: 1.4g; Protein: 16.1g

French Toast Breakfast Sandwich

Prep Time: 15 Minutes   Cook Time: 5 Minutes   Serves: 2

Preparation and Cooking Tips: You can also add a drizzle of paprika on top of the filling.

Serving Suggestion: Serve the sandwich with crispy

bacon and your favorite sauce on the side.

Ingredients:

- 4 slices white bread, cut in a 4-inch circle
- ½ teaspoon cinnamon
- Dash of nutmeg
- 2 tablespoons butter
- 2 beaten eggs
- ¼ cup milk

Filling:

- 4 tablespoons maple syrup
- 4 bacon slices
- 2 eggs, beaten

Directions:

1. In a bowl, combine the eggs, milk, cinnamon, and nutmeg; mix well. Coat each bread slice with the mixture.
2. Preheat the Breakfast Sandwich Maker until the green PREHEAT light comes on.
3. Lift cover, top rings, and cooking plates.
4. Brush one bread slice with the 1 tablespoon butter, place it in the sandwich maker, and top it with ½ of the bacon strip.
5. Lower the cooking plate and top rings then pour in ½ of the eggs on top.
6. Add the other circle of the bread on top.
7. Cover the top hood, and let the sandwich cook for 5 minutes.
8. When finished cooking, rotate the handle of the cooking plate clockwise until it stops.
9. Lift the hood, and the rings and transfer the sandwich to a plate.

Nutritional Value (Amount per Serving):

Calories: 354; Fat: 7.9g; Sodium: 704mg; Carbs: 6g; Fiber: 3.6g; Sugar: 6g; Protein: 18g

Cheddar and Ham Biscuit Sandwiches

Prep Time: 15 Minutes   Cook Time: 5 Minutes   Serves: 8

Preparation and Cooking Tips: Add a layer of pickled veggies for a change of taste.

Serving Suggestion: Would you please serve the sandwich with crispy fries on the side?

Ingredients:

- 12 tablespoons grated sharp cheddar cheese

- 8 tablespoons black mission fig jam
- 8 biscuits, cut in half
- 8 teaspoons butter
- 12 ounces sliced ham
- ½ cup Heirloom grits

Directions:

1. Preheat the Breakfast Sandwich Maker until the green PREHEAT light comes on.
2. Lift cover, top rings, and cooking plates.
3. Place half of the biscuit, cut-side up, inside the bottom tray of the sandwich maker.
4. Spread the 1 teaspoon butter and 1 tablespoon jam on top of the biscuit half.
5. Lower the cooking plate and top rings, then add ⅛ of the ham, grits, and cheese.
6. Place the other half of the biscuit on top. Cover the top hood, and let the sandwich cook for 5 minutes.
7. Rotate the handle of the cooking plate clockwise until it stops.
8. Lift the hood, and the rings and transfer the sandwich to a plate.
9. Use the remaining biscuits and ingredients to make more sandwiches in the same way.

Nutritional Value (Amount per Serving):

Calories: 312; Fat: 25g; Sodium: 132mg; Carbs: 4g; Fiber: 3.9g; Sugar: 3g; Protein: 18.9g

Cheese Egg Muffins

Prep Time: 15 Minutes   Cook Time: 5 Minutes   Serves: 2

Preparation and Cooking Tips: Add a layer of pickled veggies for a change of taste.

Serving Suggestion: Would you please serve the sandwich with crispy fries on the side?

Ingredients:

- 1 red onion, peeled, separated into rings
- 2 whole-grain English muffins, toasted
- 2 ounces sharp cheddar cheese, sliced
- 2 tablespoons green hot sauce
- 1 tablespoon unsalted butter
- 1 teaspoon soy sauce
- ½ teaspoon garlic powder
- 2 tablespoons olive oil
- ¼ cup soft herbs, chopped
- 4 large eggs, beaten
- Salt, to taste

Directions:

1. Toss onion with soy sauce, garlic powder, olive oil, salt, herbs, and sauce in a bowl.
2. Preheat the Breakfast Sandwich Maker until the green PREHEAT light comes on.
3. Lift cover, top rings, and cooking plates. Place half of the English muffin, cut side up, inside the bottom tray of the sandwich maker.
4. Brush its top with butter and add ½ of the onion mixture.
5. Lower the cooking plate and top rings, then pour in ½ of the egg.
6. Place the cheese and other top half of the muffin on top and brush it with butter. Cover the top hood, and let the muffin cook for 5 minutes.
7. Rotate the handle of the cooking plate clockwise until it stops.
8. Lift the hood, and the rings and transfer the muffin to a plate.
9. Repeat the same steps with the remaining ingredients as well.

Nutritional Value (Amount per Serving):

Calories: 404; Fat: 13g; Sodium: 216mg; Carbs: 7g; Fiber: 3g; Sugar: 4g; Protein: 31g

Cheddar and Ham Muffin

Prep Time: 15 Minutes   Cook Time: 5 Minutes   Serves: 1

Preparation and Cooking Tips: Add some additional ground black pepper to the filling.

Serving Suggestion: Serve the sandwich with crispy bacon and your favorite sauce on the side.

Ingredients:

- 1 toasted English muffin, sliced
- 1 slice of cheddar cheese
- 1 large egg, beaten
- 2 slices deli ham

Directions:

1. Preheat the Breakfast Sandwich Maker until the green PREHEAT light comes on.
2. Lift cover, top rings, and cooking plates.
3. Place the lower half of the muffin in the sandwich maker and top it with ham slices.
4. Now lower the cooking plate and top rings, then pour in the egg.
5. Place the cheese slice and the top half of the bun on top.
6. Cover the top hood, and let the sandwich cook for 5 minutes.
7. When finished cooking, rotate the handle of the cooking plate clockwise until it stops.
8. Lift the hood, and the rings and transfer the sandwich to a plate.

Nutritional Value (Amount per Serving):

Calories: 307; Fat: 8.6g; Sodium: 510mg; Carbs: 22.2g; Fiber: 1.4g; Sugar: 13g; Protein: 33.6g

Chapter 7: Vegetarian Sandwiches

Chocolate-Nut Sandwich

Prep Time: 15 Minutes   Cook Time: 5 Minutes   Serves: 2

Preparation and Cooking Tips: Add some additional dried herbs to the filling.

Serving Suggestion: Would you please serve the sandwich with crispy bacon and your favorite sauce on the side?

Ingredients:

- 4 slices whole-wheat bread, cut into a 4-inch circle
- ¼ cup roasted macadamia nuts, chopped
- 6 squares of white chocolate, slightly crushed
- ½ teaspoons light butter

Directions:

1. Make two sandwiches with sprinkles of macadamia chops and white chocolate bits.
2. Preheat the Breakfast Sandwich Maker until the green PREHEAT light comes on.
3. Lift cover, top rings, and cooking plates. Place a sandwich in the sandwich maker.
4. Lightly pat butter on each sandwich maker pan.
5. Now lower the cooking plate and top rings.
6. Cover the top hood, and let the sandwich cook for 5 minutes.
7. When finished cooking, rotate the handle of the cooking plate clockwise until it stops.
8. Lift the hood, and the rings and transfer the sandwich to a plate.
9. Repeat the same steps with the remaining ingredients.

Nutritional Value (Amount per Serving):

Calories: 149; Fat: 1.2g; Sodium: 3mg; Carbs: 37.6g; Fiber: 5.8g; Sugar: 29g; Protein: 1.1g

Jackfruit and Cabbage Burger

Prep Time: 15 Minutes   Cook Time: 25 Minutes   Serves: 2

Preparation and Cooking Tips: you can also add a lettuce leaf to the filling.

Serving Suggestion: Serve the sandwich with a cauliflower bacon salad on the side.

Ingredients:

- 5 tablespoons jerk barbecue marinade
- 1 tablespoon chopped fresh coriander
- 5 tablespoons vegan mayonnaise
- 2 vegan burger buns, cut in half
- ¼ red cabbage, shredded
- 1 carrot, peeled and ribboned
- 2 spring onions, chopped
- ½ lb. tin jackfruit
- Salt and black pepper

Directions:

1. Mix jackfruits with jerk barbecue marinade, coriander, cabbage, carrot, black pepper, salt, and spring onions on a baking sheet.
2. At 350 degrees F, preheat your oven. Bake the jackfruit mixture for 20 minutes then shred it with a fork.
3. Preheat the Breakfast Sandwich Maker until the green PREHEAT light comes on. Lift cover, top rings, and cooking plates.
4. Place half of a bun, cut-side up, inside the bottom tray of the sandwich maker.
5. Add ½ of the mayonnaise and jackfruit. Now lower the cooking plate and top rings.
6. Place the other half of the muffin on top. Cover the top hood, and let the burger cook for 5 minutes.
7. Rotate the handle of the cooking plate clockwise until it stops.
8. Lift the hood, and the rings and transfer the burger to a plate.
9. Repeat the same steps with the remaining ingredients.

Nutritional Value (Amount per Serving):

Calories: 282; Fat: 15g; Sodium: 526mg; Carbs: 20g; Fiber: 0.6g; Sugar: 3.3g; Protein: 16g

Egg Cheddar Cheese Biscuit

Prep Time: 15 Minutes   Cook Time: 5 Minutes   Serves: 1

Preparation and Cooking Tips: Add some additional dried herbs to the filling.

Serving Suggestion: Serve the sandwich with your favorite sauce on the side.

Ingredients:

- 1 slice green pepper, seeded and cored
- 1 slice of cheddar cheese
- 1 biscuit, sliced
- 1 slice red onion
- 1 large egg, beaten

Directions:

1. Top the biscuit with a slice of cheddar cheese along

with the red onion and green pepper.

2. Slide the egg tray into place and crack the egg into it.
3. Top the egg with the other top half of the biscuit.
4. Preheat the Breakfast Sandwich Maker until the green PREHEAT light comes on.
5. Lift cover, top rings, and cooking plates. Place one biscuit round in the sandwich maker.
6. Top it with pepper and onion. Now lower the cooking plate and top rings, then pour the egg on top and place a cheese slice.
7. Add the other circle of the biscuit on top. Cover the top hood, and let the sandwich cook for 5 minutes.
8. When finished cooking, rotate the handle of the cooking plate clockwise until it stops.
9. Lift the hood, and the rings and transfer the sandwich to a plate.

Nutritional Value (Amount per Serving):

Calories: 496; Fat: 20.5g; Sodium: 1885mg; Carbs: 6.5g; Fiber: 0.3g; Sugar: 5.2g; Protein: 67.7g

Maple Apple Sandwich

Prep Time: 15 Minutes   Cook Time: 5 Minutes   Serves: 2

Preparation and Cooking Tips: Add some additional dried herbs to the filling.

Serving Suggestion: Serve the sandwich with crispy bacon and your favorite sauce on the side.

Ingredients:

- 4 slices whole-wheat bread, cut in a 4-inch circle
- 1 teaspoon ground cinnamon
- 2 teaspoons pure maple syrup
- ½ teaspoons light butter
- ½ apple, sliced

Directions:

1. Spread maple syrup on each bread slice.
2. Make two sandwiches, layering apple slices, and sprinkles of cinnamon powder.
3. Preheat the Breakfast Sandwich Maker until the green PREHEAT light comes on.
4. Lift cover, top rings, and cooking plates. Lightly pat butter on each sandwich maker pan.
5. Place a sandwich in the sandwich maker.
6. Now lower the cooking plate and top rings. Cover the top hood, and let the sandwich cook for 5 minutes.

7. When finished cooking, rotate the handle of the cooking plate clockwise until it stops.
8. Lift the hood, and the rings and transfer the sandwich to a plate.
9. Repeat the same steps with the remaining ingredients.

Nutritional Value (Amount per Serving):

Calories: 266; Fat: 11.8g; Sodium: 267mg; Carbs: 37.6g; Fiber: 2.3g; Sugar: 5g; Protein: 2.2g

Cheese and Raspberry Nutella Sandwich

Prep Time: 15 Minutes   Cook Time: 5 Minutes   Serves: 2

Preparation and Cooking Tips: You can also add a drizzle of chocolate chips to the filling.

Serving Suggestion: Would you please serve the sandwich with a banana smoothie on the side?

Ingredients:

- 4 brown bread slices, cut into 4 inches round
- 2 tablespoons raspberry preserves
- 2 tablespoon Nutella spread
- ½ fresh raspberries, sliced
- 2 tablespoons cream cheese

Directions:

1. Preheat the Breakfast Sandwich Maker until the green PREHEAT light comes on.
2. Lift cover, top rings, and cooking plates.
3. Place a bread slice, inside the bottom tray of the sandwich maker.
4. Spread ½ of the preserves, Nutella, raspberries, and cream cheese on top.
5. Place the other bread slice on top. Now lower the cooking plate and top rings then.
6. Cover the top hood, and let the sandwich cook for 5 minutes.
7. Rotate the handle of the cooking plate clockwise until it stops.
8. Lift the hood, and the rings and transfer the sandwich to a plate.
9. Repeat the same steps with the remaining ingredients.

Nutritional Value (Amount per Serving):

Calories: 282; Fat: 15g; Sodium: 526mg; Carbs: 20g; Fiber: 0.6g; Sugar: 3.3g; Protein: 16g

Kiwi, Strawberry, and Orange Sandwich

Prep Time: 15 Minutes   Cook Time: 5 Minutes   Serves: 2

Preparation and Cooking Tips: You can also add a drizzle of chocolate chips to the filling.

Serving Suggestion: Would you please serve the sandwich with an apple smoothie on the side?

Ingredients:

- 4 slices shokunin (Japanese Pullman loaf bread), cut into 4 inches round
- 12 strawberries, sliced
- 1 navel orange, sliced
- 2 kiwis, sliced

Whipped cream:

- 1 cup heavy whipping cream
- 5 teaspoons sugar
- 1 teaspoon rum

Directions:

1. Beat cream with rum and sugar in a bowl.
2. Preheat the Breakfast Sandwich Maker until the green PREHEAT light comes on.
3. Lift cover, top rings, and cooking plates.
4. Place a bread slice inside the bottom tray of the sandwich maker.
5. Add ½ of the cream, orange, kiwi and strawberry. Place the other bread slice on top.
6. Lower the cooking plate and top rings then pour in the egg. Cover the top hood, and let the sandwich cook for 5 minutes.
7. Rotate the handle of the cooking plate clockwise until it stops.
8. Lift the hood, and the rings and transfer the sandwich to a plate.
9. Repeat the same steps with the remaining ingredients.

Nutritional Value (Amount per Serving):

Calories: 284; Fat: 16g; Sodium: 252mg; Carbs: 31.6g; Fiber: 0.9g; Sugar: 6.6g; Protein: 3.7g

Cucumber, Avocado, and Broccoli Sandwich

Prep Time: 15 Minutes   Cook Time: 5 Minutes   Serves: 2

Preparation and Cooking Tips: Add a layer of sliced bell peppers for a change of taste.

Serving Suggestion: Would you please serve the sandwich with a broccoli salad on the side?

Ingredients:

- 4 slices thin-sliced bread, cut into 4 inches rounds
- ½ avocado, peeled and sliced
- 2 tablespoons plain hummus
- ⅛ teaspoon kosher salt
- ½ cup broccoli sprouts
- 8 slices tomato
- 8 slices cucumber

Directions:

1. Preheat the Breakfast Sandwich Maker until the green PREHEAT light comes on.
2. Lift cover, top rings, and cooking plates.
3. Place a bread slice inside the bottom tray of the sandwich maker.
4. Spread ½ of the hummus, salt, tomato, avocado, cucumber, and broccoli on top.
5. Now lower the cooking plate and top rings. Place another bread slice on top.
6. Cover the top hood, and let the sandwich cook for 5 minutes.
7. Rotate the handle of the cooking plate clockwise until it stops.
8. Lift the hood, and the rings and transfer the sandwich to a plate.
9. Repeat the same steps with the remaining ingredients.

Nutritional Value (Amount per Serving):

Calories: 113; Fat: 3g; Sodium: 152mg; Carbs: 20g; Fiber: 3g; Sugar: 1.1g; Protein: 3.5g

Margherita Flatbread Sandwiches

Prep Time: 15 Minutes   Cook Time: 5 Minutes   Serves: 2

Preparation and Cooking Tips: You can also add a drizzle of paprika on top of the filling.

Serving Suggestion: Serve the sandwich with your favorite sauce on the side.

Ingredients:

- 1 round flatbread, cut into 4-inch circle
- 2 teaspoons grated parmesan cheese
- 1 teaspoon olive oil

- 1 garlic clove, minced
- 1 slice of mozzarella cheese
- 2 thin slices of ripe tomato
- 1 thin slice of red onion
- 4 fresh basil leaves
- Pinch dried oregano
- 1 large egg, beaten

Directions:

1. Preheat the Breakfast Sandwich Maker until the green PREHEAT light comes on.
2. Lift cover, top rings, and cooking plates.
3. Place the lower half of the muffin in the sandwich maker. Brush the flatbread with the olive oil and sprinkle with garlic.
4. Add ½ of the tomatoes, red onion, and basil leaves, then sprinkle with dried oregano.
5. Top the vegetables with ½ of the mozzarella cheese. Now lower the cooking plate and top rings, and pour the egg in it.
6. Add the other circle of the bread on top. Cover the top hood, and let the sandwich cook for 5 minutes.
7. When finished cooking, rotate the handle of the cooking plate clockwise until it stops.
8. Lift the hood, and the rings and transfer the sandwich to a plate. Sprinkle the sandwich with parmesan cheese then enjoy.
9. Repeat the same steps with the remaining ingredients.

Nutritional Value (Amount per Serving):

Calories: 336; Fat: 12.8g; Sodium: 40mg; Carbs: 4.2g; Fiber: 1g; Sugar: 0.7g; Protein: 50.7g

Veggie Burgers

Prep Time: 15 Minutes   Cook Time: 15 Minutes   Serves: 3

Preparation and Cooking Tips: Add a layer of sliced bell peppers for a change of taste.

Serving Suggestion: Serve the sandwich with a cauliflower bacon salad on the side.

Ingredients:

- 3 medium potatoes, half-boiled, peeled and grated
- 1 (15-ounce) can black beans, drained
- 1 medium carrot, grated
- ½ medium onion, chopped
- 4 large scallions, chopped
- ½ teaspoon garlic salt

- 2 tablespoons olive oil
- 1 cup corn, fresh

Directions:

1. Blend black beans with onion, corn, scallions, salt, and carrots in a food processor for 1 minute.
2. Make 3 equal-sized patties out of the turkey mixture. Set a suitable skillet with olive oil over medium-high heat. Sear the bean patties in the oil for 5 minutes per side.
3. Preheat the Breakfast Sandwich Maker until the green PREHEAT light comes on.
4. Lift cover, top rings, and cooking plates. Add ⬚ of the grated potato, inside the bottom tray of the sandwich maker.
5. Lower the cooking plate and top rings then place a bean patty on top.
6. Place ⬚ of the grated potatoes on top and drizzle oil on top. Cover the top hood, and let the burger cook for 5 minutes.
7. Rotate the handle of the cooking plate clockwise until it stops.
8. Lift the hood, and the rings and transfer the burger to a plate.
9. Repeat the same steps with the remaining ingredients.

Nutritional Value (Amount per Serving):

Calories: 237; Fat: 19g; Sodium: 518mg; Carbs: 7g; Fiber: 1.5g; Sugar: 3.4g; Protein: 12g

Apple Sandwich with Strawberry Jam

Prep Time: 15 Minutes   Cook Time: 5 Minutes   Serves: 2

Preparation and Cooking Tips: You can also add a drizzle of lemon juice on top of the filling.

Serving Suggestion: Serve the sandwich with your favorite sauce on the side.

Ingredients:

- 4 slices whole-wheat bread, cut into a 4-inch circle
- 1 tablespoon strawberry jam
- ½ teaspoons light butter
- ½ apple, sliced

Directions:

1. Preheat the Breakfast Sandwich Maker until the green PREHEAT light comes on.

2. Lift cover, top rings, and cooking plates.
3. Place a bread round in the sandwich maker.
4. Spread ½ of the butter and jam on top.
5. Lower the cooking plate and top rings, then place ½ of the apple, and another bread slice on top.
6. Cover the top hood, and let the sandwich cook for 5 minutes.
7. When finished cooking, rotate the handle of the cooking plate clockwise until it stops.
8. Lift the hood, and the rings and transfer the sandwich to a plate.
9. Repeat the same steps with the remaining ingredients.

Nutritional Value (Amount per Serving):

Calories: 198; Fat: 14g; Sodium: 272mg; Carbs: 34g; Fiber: 1g; Sugar: 9.3g; Protein: 1.3g

Florentine Biscuit with Yogurt

Prep Time: 15 Minutes   Cook Time: 7 Minutes   Serves: 1

Preparation and Cooking Tips: Add some additional dried herbs to the filling.

Serving Suggestion: Serve the sandwich with coleslaw and your favorite sauce on the side.

Ingredients:

- 2 slices multigrain bread, cut into a 4-inch circle
- 1 tablespoon minced yellow onion
- 2 tablespoons plain nonfat yogurt
- ¼ teaspoon Dijon mustard
- 1 large egg, beaten
- ½ cup baby spinach
- 1 teaspoon olive oil

Directions:

1. Heat the oil in a suitable skillet over medium heat. Add the onion and spinach and stir well. Cook for almost 2 minutes, stirring, until the spinach is just wilted. Set aside.
2. Preheat the Breakfast Sandwich Maker until the green PREHEAT light comes on.
3. Lift cover, top rings, and cooking plates. Place one bread slice in the sandwich maker.
4. Whisk together the yogurt and mustard in a small bowl, then brush over the piece of bread.
5. Top the bread with the cooked spinach and onion mixture.
6. Now lower the cooking plate and top rings, then

pour in the egg.
7. Add the other circle of the bread on top. Cover the top hood, and let the sandwich cook for 5 minutes.
8. When finished cooking, rotate the handle of the cooking plate clockwise until it stops.
9. Lift the hood, and the rings and transfer the sandwich to a plate.

Nutritional Value (Amount per Serving):

Calories: 305; Fat: 12.7g; Sodium: 227mg; Carbs: 26.1g; Fiber: 1.4g; Sugar: 0.9g; Protein: 35.2g

Apple, Cinnamon and Raisin Sandwich

Prep Time: 15 Minutes   Cook Time: 5 Minutes   Serves: 1

Preparation and Cooking Tips: You can also add lettuce leaves to the filling.

Serving Suggestion: Serve the sandwich with coleslaw and your favorite sauce on the side.

Ingredients:

- ½ medium granny smith apple, sliced
- 1 slice of sharp cheddar cheese
- 1 cinnamon raisin bagel

Directions:

1. Preheat the Breakfast Sandwich Maker until the green PREHEAT light comes on.
2. Lift cover, top rings, and cooking plates.
3. Place the lower half of the bagel in the sandwich maker.
4. Top the bottom of the bagel with the thin slices of apple.
5. Place the slice of sharp cheddar cheese on top of the apple slices.
6. Now lower the cooking plate and top rings. Place the other half of the bagel on top.
7. Cover the top hood, and let the sandwich cook for 5 minutes.
8. When finished cooking, rotate the handle of the cooking plate clockwise until it stops.
9. Lift the hood, and the rings and transfer the sandwich to a plate.

Nutritional Value (Amount per Serving):

Calories: 284; Fat: 16g; Sodium: 252mg; Carbs: 31.6g; Fiber: 0.9g; Sugar: 6.6g; Protein: 3.7g

Dark Chocolate and Cherries Sandwich

Prep Time: 15 Minutes   Cook Time: 5 Minutes   Serves: 2

Preparation and Cooking Tips: Add some additional dried herbs to the filling.

Serving Suggestion: Serve the sandwich with crispy bacon and your favorite sauce on the side.

Ingredients:

- 6 squares of dark chocolate 70% cocoa, slightly crushed
- 4 slices whole-wheat bread, cut into a 4-inch circle
- ¼ cup cherries, slightly crushed
- ½ teaspoons light butter

Directions:

1. Mix the cherries and dark chocolate.
2. Make two sandwiches with the chocolate and cherry mixture.
3. Preheat the Breakfast Sandwich Maker until the green PREHEAT light comes on.
4. Lift cover, top rings, and cooking plates.
5. Lightly pat butter on each sandwich maker pan. Place a sandwich in the sandwich maker.
6. Now lower the cooking plate and top rings. Cover the top hood, and let the sandwich cook for 5 minutes.
7. When finished cooking, rotate the handle of the cooking plate clockwise until it stops.
8. Lift the hood, and the rings and transfer the sandwich to a plate.
9. Repeat the same steps with the remaining ingredients.

Nutritional Value (Amount per Serving):

Calories: 186; Fat: 9g; Sodium: 124mg; Carbs: 23g; Fiber: 0.4g; Sugar: 11.5g; Protein: 3.2 g

Sweet Mango and Peach Sandwich

Prep Time: 15 Minutes   Cook Time: 5 Minutes   Serves: 2

Preparation and Cooking Tips: Add some additional ground black pepper to the filling.

Serving Suggestion: Serve the sandwich with your favorite sauce on the side.

Ingredients:

- 4 slices whole-wheat bread, cut into a 4-inch circle
- 2 teaspoons pure maple syrup or wild honey
- ½ teaspoons light butter
- ½ mango, sliced
- 1 peach, sliced

Directions:

1. Spread the honey or maple syrup on each bread slice.
2. Make two sandwiches, layering mango and peach slices.
3. Preheat the Breakfast Sandwich Maker until the green PREHEAT light comes on.
4. Lift cover, top rings, and cooking plates.
5. Lightly pat butter on each sandwich maker pan. Place a sandwich in the sandwich maker.
6. Now lower the cooking plate and top rings. Cover the top hood, and let the sandwich cook for 5 minutes.
7. When finished cooking, rotate the handle of the cooking plate clockwise until it stops.
8. Lift the hood, and the rings and transfer the sandwich to a plate.
9. Repeat the same steps with the remaining ingredients.

Nutritional Value (Amount per Serving):

Calories: 297; Fat: 2.1g; Sodium: 248.1mg; Carbs: 64.9g; Fiber: 3.9g; Sugar: 9g; Protein: 5.5g

Cheese and Salami Sandwich

Prep Time: 15 Minutes   Cook Time: 5 Minutes   Serves: 1

Preparation and Cooking Tips: You can also add a layer of your favorite sauce to the filling.

Serving Suggestion: Serve the sandwich with crispy bacon and your favorite sauce on the side.

Ingredients:

- 2 slices thick white bread, cut into a 4-inch circle
- 1 tablespoon roasted red pepper, chopped
- 1 tablespoon chopped black olives
- 1 teaspoon minced red onion
- 1 slice provolone cheese
- 1 slice deli ham
- 1 slice of hard salami
- 1 garlic clove, minced
- Salt and black pepper
- 1 large egg

Directions:

1. Stir together the olives, red pepper, red onion and garlic. Season with salt and black pepper and stir well.
2. Preheat the Breakfast Sandwich Maker until the green PREHEAT light comes on.
3. Lift cover, top rings, and cooking plates. Place one of the bread slices in the sandwich maker.
4. Layer the ham and salami over the bread and top with the olive mixture.
5. Top the olive mixture with a slice of provolone cheese.
6. Now lower the cooking plate and top rings, and crack the egg in it.
7. Add the other circle of the bread on top. Cover the top hood, and let the sandwich cook for 5 minutes.
8. When finished cooking, rotate the handle of the cooking plate clockwise until it stops.
9. Lift the hood, and the rings and transfer the sandwich to a plate.

Nutritional Value (Amount per Serving):

Calories: 361; Fat: 16g; Sodium: 515mg; Carbs: 19.3g; Fiber: 0.1g; Sugar: 18.2g; Protein: 33.3g

Garlic Tomato and Black Bean Burgers

Prep Time: 15 Minutes   Cook Time: 15 Minutes   Serves: 4

Preparation and Cooking Tips: Add a layer of pickled onions for a change of taste.

Serving Suggestion: Serve the sandwich with crispy zucchini fries on the side.

Ingredients:

- 1 (14-ounce) can black beans, well-drained
- 2 medium red heirloom tomatoes, sliced
- ½ medium red onion, sliced
- 2 tablespoons olive oil
- 2 slices bread, crumbled
- ½ medium onion, chopped
- ½ teaspoon seasoned salt
- 1 teaspoon garlic powder
- 1 teaspoon onion powder
- ½ cup all-purpose flour
- 6 leaves butter lettuce
- 1 dash black pepper
- 1 dash of kosher salt

- 4 buns, split

Directions:

1. Blend black beans, crumbled bread, onion, garlic powder, salt, and onion powder in a food processor for 1 minute.
2. Set a suitable skillet with olive oil over medium-high heat. Make 4 equal-sized patties out of this bean mixture. Sear the bean patties in the oil for 5 minutes per side.
3. Preheat the Breakfast Sandwich Maker until the green PREHEAT light comes on. Lift cover, top rings, and cooking plates.
4. Place half of a bun, cut-side up, inside the bottom tray of the sandwich maker.
5. Lower the cooking plate and top rings, then place a patty, a lettuce leaf, an onion slice, and a tomato slice on top.
6. Place the other half of the bun on top. Cover the top hood, and let the burger cook for 5 minutes.
7. Rotate the handle of the cooking plate clockwise until it stops.
8. Lift the hood, and the rings and transfer the burger to a plate.
9. Repeat the same steps with the remaining ingredients.

Nutritional Value (Amount per Serving):

Calories: 229; Fat: 1.9; Sodium: 567mg; Carbs: 1.9g; Fiber: 0.4g; Sugar: 0.6g; Protein: 11.8g

Pistachio Baklava Sandwich

Prep Time: 15 Minutes   Cook Time: 5 Minutes   Serves: 2

Preparation and Cooking Tips: You can also add a layer of your favorite sauce to the filling.

Serving Suggestion: Serve the sandwich with crispy bacon and your favorite sauce on the side.

Ingredients:

- 4 slices whole-wheat bread, cut into a 4-inch circle
- ½ teaspoons ground cinnamon
- ½ teaspoons light butter
- ¼ cup pistachios, crushed
- 2 teaspoons wild honey

Directions:

1. Preheat the Breakfast Sandwich Maker until the green PREHEAT light comes on.
2. Lift cover, top rings, and cooking plates. Lightly pat

butter on each sandwich maker pan.

3. Mix the pistachios, wild honey, and cinnamon. Make two sandwiches with the pistachio mixture.
4. Place a sandwich in the sandwich maker. Now lower the cooking plate and top rings.
5. Cover the top hood, and let the sandwich cook for 5 minutes.
6. When finished cooking, rotate the handle of the cooking plate clockwise until it stops.
7. Lift the hood, and the rings and transfer the sandwich to a plate.
8. Repeat the same steps with the remaining ingredients.

Nutritional Value (Amount per Serving):

Calories: 250; Fat: 13.6g; Sodium: 99mg; Carbs: 30.7g; Fiber: 0.4g; Sugar: 22.1g; Protein: 2.4g

Peach Bran Sandwich

Prep Time: 15 Minutes   Cook Time: 5 Minutes   Serves: 2

Preparation and Cooking Tips: You can also add a drizzle of chocolate chips to the filling.

Serving Suggestion: Serve the sandwich with a glass of orange juice on the side.

Ingredients:

- 4 bran bread slices, cut into 4 inches round
- 2 tablespoons peach preserves
- 1 peach, peeled and sliced

Directions:

1. Preheat the Breakfast Sandwich Maker until the green PREHEAT light comes on.
2. Lift cover, top rings, and cooking plates.
3. Place a bread slice, inside the bottom tray of the sandwich maker.
4. Spread ½ of the preserves, and peach slices on top.
5. Now lower the cooking plate and top rings. Place the other bread slice on top.
6. Cover the top hood, and let the sandwich cook for 5 minutes.
7. Rotate the handle of the cooking plate clockwise until it stops.
8. Lift the hood, and the rings and transfer the sandwich to a plate.
9. Repeat the same steps with the remaining ingredients.

Nutritional Value (Amount per Serving):

Calories: 282; Fat: 15g; Sodium: 526mg; Carbs: 20g; Fiber: 0.6g; Sugar: 3.3g; Protein: 16g

Cheese and Egg Seed Bagel

Prep Time: 15 Minutes   Cook Time: 5 Minutes   Serves: 1

Preparation and Cooking Tips: You can also add lettuce leaves to the filling.

Serving Suggestion: Serve the sandwich with your favorite sauce on the side.

Ingredients:

- 1 poppy seed bagel, sliced
- 1 teaspoon chopped chives
- 1-ounce goat cheese
- 1 large egg
- Salt and black pepper

Directions:

1. Beat the egg with chopped chives, salt and pepper.
2. Preheat the Breakfast Sandwich Maker until the green PREHEAT light comes on.
3. Lift cover, top rings, and cooking plates.
4. Place the lower half of the bagel in the sandwich maker. Layer the goat cheese on top of the bagel.
5. Now lower the cooking plate and top rings, then pour in the egg mixture.
6. Place the other half of the bagel on top.
7. Cover the top hood, and let the sandwich cook for 5 minutes.
8. When finished cooking, rotate the handle of the cooking plate clockwise until it stops.
9. Lift the hood, and the rings and transfer the sandwich to a plate.

Nutritional Value (Amount per Serving):

Calories: 354; Fat: 7.9g; Sodium: 704mg; Carbs: 6g; Fiber: 3.6g; Sugar: 6g; Protein: 18g

Mushroom and Cucumber Panini

Prep Time: 15 Minutes   Cook Time: 5 Minutes   Serves: 2

Preparation and Cooking Tips: You can also add lettuce leaves to the filling.

Serving Suggestion: Serve the sandwich with crispy bacon and your favorite sauce on the side.

Ingredients:

- ¼ cup Brianna's Real French Vinaigrette Dressing

- 4 Portobello mushroom caps, pressed
- 1 small seedless cucumber, sliced
- 4 ounces sliced black olives, drained
- 1 green bell pepper, chopped
- 1 small onion, quartered
- 1 red bell pepper, chopped

Directions:

1. Mix all cucumber and all the veggies in a bowl with the dressing.
2. Preheat the Breakfast Sandwich Maker until the green PREHEAT light comes on.
3. Lift cover, top rings, and cooking plates.
4. Place one circle of the mushroom in the sandwich maker.
5. Top it with ½ of the veggie mixture. Now lower the cooking plate and top rings.
6. Add the other circle of the mushroom on top. Cover the top hood, and let the sandwich cook for 5 minutes.
7. When finished cooking, rotate the handle of the cooking plate clockwise until it stops.
8. Lift the hood, and the rings and transfer the sandwich to a plate.
9. Repeat the same with the remaining ingredients.

Nutritional Value (Amount per Serving):

Calories: 395; Fat: 9.5g; Sodium: 655mg; Carbs: 3.4g; Fiber: 0.4g; Sugar: 0.4g; Protein: 28.3g

Aioli Avocado, Bacon, and Cheddar Sandwich

Prep Time: 15 Minutes   Cook Time: 5 Minutes   Serves: 1

Preparation and Cooking Tips: You can also add lettuce leaves to the filling.

Serving Suggestion: Serve the sandwich with your favorite sauce on the side.

Ingredients:

- 2 slices multi-grain bread, cut into a 4-inch circle
- 2 slices thick-cut bacon, cooked
- 1 slice sharp cheddar
- ¼ avocado, sliced
- 1 slice red onion
- 1 tablespoon Aioli
- 1 large egg

Directions:

1. Preheat the Breakfast Sandwich Maker until the green PREHEAT light comes on.
2. Lift cover, top rings, and cooking plates.
3. Place one bread slice in the sandwich maker and top it with bacon, avocado, onion and aioli.
4. Now lower the cooking plate and top rings, then pour in the egg.
5. Add the cheese and another circle of the bread on top.
6. Cover the top hood, and let the sandwich cook for 5 minutes.
7. When finished cooking, rotate the handle of the cooking plate clockwise until it stops.
8. Lift the hood, and the rings and transfer the sandwich to a plate.

Nutritional Value (Amount per Serving):

Calories: 327; Fat: 14.2g; Sodium: 672mg; Carbs: 47.2g; Fiber: 1.7g; Sugar: 24.8g; Protein: 4.4g

Black Bean Salsa Burger

Prep Time: 15 Minutes   Cook Time: 15 Minutes   Serves: 8

Preparation and Cooking Tips: Add a layer of spicy mayo and pickled veggies for a change of taste.

Serving Suggestion: Serve the sandwich with crispy sweet potato fries on the side.

Ingredients:

- 2 (15-ounce) cans of black beans, drained
- 8 hamburger buns, split in half
- ½ cup whole wheat flour
- ¼ cup yellow cornmeal
- 2 teaspoons ground cumin
- 1 teaspoon garlic salt
- ½ cup salsa

Directions:

1. Blend beans with whole wheat flour, cornmeal, salsa, cumin, and salt in a food processor for 1 minute.
2. Set a suitable skillet with olive oil over medium-high heat. Make 8 equal-sized patties out of the bean mixture. Sear the bean patties in the oil for 5 minutes per side.
3. Preheat the Breakfast Sandwich Maker until the green PREHEAT light comes on. Lift cover, top rings, and cooking plates.
4. Place half of a bun, cut-side up, inside the bottom

tray of the sandwich maker.

5. Lower the cooking plate and top rings, then place a patty on top.
6. Place the other half of the bun on top. Cover the top hood, and let the burger cook for 5 minutes.
7. Rotate the handle of the cooking plate clockwise until it stops.
8. Lift the hood, and the rings and transfer the burger to a plate.
9. Repeat the same steps with the remaining ingredients.

Nutritional Value (Amount per Serving):

Calories: 209; Fat: 7.5g; Sodium: 321mg; Carbs: 34.1g; Fiber: 4g; Sugar: 3.8g; Protein: 4.3g

Homemade Blueberry Nutella Sandwich

Prep Time: 15 Minutes   Cook Time: 5 Minutes   Serves: 2

Preparation and Cooking Tips: You can also add a drizzle of chocolate sprinkles to the filling.

Serving Suggestion: Would you please serve the sandwich with a chocolate smoothie on the side?

Ingredients:

- 4 white bread slices, cut into 4 inches round
- 2 tablespoons blueberry preserves
- 2 tablespoon Nutella spread
- ½ fresh blueberries, sliced

Directions:

1. Preheat the Breakfast Sandwich Maker until the green PREHEAT light comes on.
2. Lift cover, top rings, and cooking plates.
3. Place a bread slice, inside the bottom tray of the sandwich maker.
4. Spread ½ of the preserves, Nutella, and blueberries on top.
5. Now lower the cooking plate and top rings. Place the other bread slice on top.
6. Cover the top hood, and let the sandwich cook for 5 minutes.
7. Rotate the handle of the cooking plate clockwise until it stops.
8. Lift the hood, and the rings and transfer the sandwich to a plate.
9. Repeat the same steps with the remaining ingredients.

Nutritional Value (Amount per Serving):

Calories: 282; Fat: 15g; Sodium: 526mg; Carbs: 20g; Fiber: 0.6g; Sugar: 3.3g; Protein: 16g

Brie Pancake and Raspberry Jam Sandwich

Prep Time: 15 Minutes   Cook Time: 5 Minutes   Serves: 1

Preparation and Cooking Tips: You can also add a drizzle of lemon juice on top of the filling.

Serving Suggestion: Serve the sandwich with crispy bacon and your favorite sauce on the side.

Ingredients:

- 1 tablespoon raspberry jam
- 1-ounce Brie, chopped
- 2 frozen pancakes
- 1 large egg

Directions:

1. Sprinkle the chopped brie on top of the pancake.
2. Slide the egg tray into place and crack the egg into it.
3. Preheat the Breakfast Sandwich Maker until the green PREHEAT light comes on.
4. Lift cover, top rings, and cooking plates.
5. Place one of the pancakes in the sandwich maker. Top it with jam and brie.
6. Lower the cooking plate and top rings, then pour in the egg.
7. Cover the top hood, and let the sandwich cook for 5 minutes.
8. When finished cooking, rotate the handle of the cooking plate clockwise until it stops.
9. Lift the hood, and the rings and transfer the sandwich to a plate.

Nutritional Value (Amount per Serving):

Calories: 315; Fat: 20.1g; Sodium: 67mg; Carbs: 1.9g; Fiber: 0.2g; Sugar: 0.7g; Protein: 30.4g

Apple Cheddar Croissant

Prep Time: 15 Minutes   Cook Time: 5 Minutes   Serves: 2

Preparation and Cooking Tips: You can also add lettuce leaves to the filling.

Serving Suggestion: Serve the sandwich with your favorite sauce on the side.

Ingredients:

- 1 small Granny Smith apple, cut into very thin rounds
- ¼ cup of shredded cheddar cheese
- 2 slices of precooked bacon
- 2 small croissants
- 2 large eggs

Directions:

1. Preheat the Breakfast Sandwich Maker until the green PREHEAT light comes on.
2. Lift cover, top rings, and cooking plates.
3. Place the lower half of the croissant in the sandwich maker. Top the croissant with ½ of the shredded cheddar cheese.
4. Place ½ of the apple slices on top of the cheese, then top with 1 slice of the precooked bacon, broken in half to make it fit on the croissant.
5. Use a whisk to whisk the two eggs together in a bowl. Now lower the cooking plate and top rings, then pour in the egg.
6. Place the other top half of the croissant on top. Cover the top hood, and let the sandwich cook for 5 minutes.
7. When finished cooking, rotate the handle of the cooking plate clockwise until it stops.
8. Lift the hood, and the rings and transfer the sandwich to a plate.
9. Repeat the same steps with the remaining ingredients.

Nutritional Value (Amount per Serving):

Calories: 251; Fat: 9g; Sodium: 412mg; Carbs: 43g; Fiber: 5.3g; Sugar: 1g; Protein: 3g

Cheese, Avocado, and Egg Sandwich

Prep Time: 15 Minutes   Cook Time: 5 Minutes   Serves: 1

Preparation and Cooking Tips: You can also add lettuce leaves to the filling.

Serving Suggestion: Serve the sandwich with your favorite sauce on the side.

Ingredients:

- ¼ ripe avocado, pitted and sliced
- 1 tablespoon sliced green onion
- 2 teaspoons half-n-half
- 1 croissant, sliced
- 2 slices ripe tomato
- 1 slice of Swiss cheese

- 1 large egg

Directions:

1. Preheat the Breakfast Sandwich Maker until the green PREHEAT light comes on.
2. Lift cover, top rings, and cooking plates.
3. Place the lower half of the croissant in the sandwich maker.
4. Top the croissant with the tomato and avocado, then top with the slice of Swiss cheese.
5. Whisk together the egg, green onion, and half-n-half in a small bowl.
6. Now lower the cooking plate and top rings, then pour in the egg.
7. Place the other top half of the croissant on top. Cover the top hood, and let the sandwich cook for 5 minutes.
8. When finished cooking, rotate the handle of the cooking plate clockwise until it stops.
9. Lift the hood, and the rings and transfer the sandwich to a plate.

Nutritional Value (Amount per Serving):

Calories: 548; Fat: 22g; Sodium: 319 mg; Carbs: 17g; Fiber: 3g; Sugar: 7.6g; Protein: 40g

Strawberry Nutella Sandwich

Prep Time: 15 Minutes   Cook Time: 5 Minutes   Serves: 2

Preparation and Cooking Tips: You can also add a drizzle of chocolate chips to the filling.

Serving Suggestion: Would you please serve the sandwich with a banana smoothie on the side?

Ingredients:

- 4 white bread slices, cut into 4 inches round
- 2 tablespoon Nutella spread
- ½ fresh strawberries, sliced
- 2 tablespoons strawberry jam

Directions:

1. Preheat the Breakfast Sandwich Maker until the green PREHEAT light comes on.
2. Lift cover, top rings, and cooking plates.
3. Place a bread slice, inside the bottom tray of the sandwich maker.
4. Spread ½ of the jam, Nutella, and strawberry on top.
5. Now lower the cooking plate and top rings.
6. Place the other bread slice on top. Cover the top hood, and let the sandwich cook for 5 minutes.

7. Rotate the handle of the cooking plate clockwise until it stops.
8. Lift the hood, and the rings and transfer the sandwich to a plate.
9. Repeat the same steps with the remaining ingredients.

Nutritional Value (Amount per Serving):

Calories: 282; Fat: 15g; Sodium: 526mg; Carbs: 20g; Fiber: 0.6g; Sugar: 3.3g, Protein: 10g

Pumpkin and Apple Sandwich

Prep Time: 15 Minutes   Cook Time: 5 Minutes   Serves: 2

Preparation and Cooking Tips: You can also add a drizzle of chocolate syrup to the filling.

Serving Suggestion: Would you please serve the sandwich with a broccoli salad on the side?

Ingredients:

- 4 whole-wheat bread slices, cut into 4 inches round
- 2 tablespoons pumpkin puree
- 2 pinches of pumpkin pie spice
- 2 tablespoon applesauce
- 1 apple, sliced

Directions:

1. Preheat the Breakfast Sandwich Maker until the green PREHEAT light comes on.
2. Lift cover, top rings, and cooking plates.
3. Place a bread slice, inside the bottom tray of the sandwich maker.
4. Spread ½ of the applesauce, pumpkin puree, a pinch of spice, and apple on top.
5. Place the other bread slice on top. Now lower the cooking plate and top rings then.
6. Cover the top hood, and let the sandwich cook for 5 minutes.
7. Rotate the handle of the cooking plate clockwise until it stops.
8. Lift the hood, and the rings and transfer the sandwich to a plate.
9. Repeat the same steps with the remaining ingredients.

Nutritional Value (Amount per Serving):

Calories: 282; Fat: 15g; Sodium: 526mg; Carbs: 20g; Fiber: 0.6g; Sugar: 3.3g; Protein: 16g

Beet and Arugula Burger

Prep Time: 15 Minutes   Cook Time: 15 Minutes   Serves: 4

Preparation and Cooking Tips: Enjoy sautéed veggies on the side for a change of taste.

Serving Suggestion: Would you please serve the sandwich with a broccoli salad on the side?

Ingredients:

- 1 cup canned black beans, rinsed and drained
- 2 tablespoons fresh parsley, chopped
- 1 large beet, peeled and quartered
- 1 shallot, peeled and quartered
- ¼ cup uncooked brown rice
- Tahini, or tzatziki, for serving
- 1 teaspoon ground cumin • 1 cup baby arugula
- ¼ teaspoon black pepper • ¾ cup water
- ¼ teaspoon kosher salt • 1 large egg
- 4 seeded buns, split • ½ cup breadcrumbs

Directions:

1. Cook rice with ¾ cup water in a saucepan until soft, then drain. Boil beet in a pot filled with water until soft then peel and chop.
2. Blend black beans with rice, egg, crumbs, parsley, cumin, beet, black pepper, and salt in a food processor for 1 minute.
3. Set a suitable skillet with olive oil over medium-high heat. Make 4 equal-sized patties out of the turkey mixture. Sear the bean patties in the oil for 5 minutes per side.
4. Preheat the Breakfast Sandwich Maker until the green PREHEAT light comes on. Lift cover, top rings, and cooking plates.
5. Place half of a bun, cut-side up, inside the bottom tray of the sandwich maker.
6. Lower the cooking plate and top rings, then place a bean patty and ¼ cup arugula on top.
7. Place the other half of the bun on top. Cover the top hood, and let the burger cook for 5 minutes.
8. Rotate the handle of the cooking plate clockwise until it stops. Lift the hood, and the rings and transfer the burger to a plate.
9. Repeat the same steps with the remaining ingredients.

Nutritional Value (Amount per Serving):

Calories: 199; Fat: 11.1g; Sodium: 297mg; Carbs: 14.9g; Fiber: 1g; Sugar: 2.5g; Protein: 9.9g

Nutella Apple Sandwich with Jam

Prep Time: 15 Minutes   Cook Time: 5 Minutes   Serves: 2

Preparation and Cooking Tips: You can also add a drizzle of chocolate syrup to the filling.

Serving Suggestion: Would you please serve the sandwich with a glass of green smoothie on the side?

Ingredients:

- 4 brown bread slices, cut into 4 inches round
- 2 tablespoon Nutella spread
- 2 tablespoon jam
- 1 apple, sliced

Directions:

1. Preheat the Breakfast Sandwich Maker until the green PREHEAT light comes on.
2. Lift cover, top rings, and cooking plates.
3. Place a bread slice, inside the bottom tray of the sandwich maker.
4. Spread ½ of the jam, Nutella, and apple on top.
5. Now lower the cooking plate and top rings.
6. Place the other bread slice on top. Cover the top hood, and let the sandwich cook for 5 minutes.
7. Rotate the handle of the cooking plate clockwise until it stops.
8. Lift the hood, and the rings and transfer the sandwich to a plate.
9. Repeat the same steps with the remaining ingredients.

Nutritional Value (Amount per Serving):

Calories: 282; Fat: 15g; Sodium: 526mg; Carbs: 20g; Fiber: 0.6g; Sugar: 3.3g; Protein: 16g

Tempeh and Carrot Sandwich

Prep Time: 15 Minutes   Cook Time: 15 Minutes   Serves: 2

Preparation and Cooking Tips: Add a layer of pickled veggies for a change of taste.

Serving Suggestion: Serve the sandwich with crispy bacon and your favorite sauce on the side.

Ingredients:

- 2 large carrots, washed and peeled
- 1 (8 ounces) package of tempeh, sliced
- 4 slices bread, cut into 4 inches round
- 2 large beefsteak tomatoes, sliced
- 4 tablespoons vegan mayo
- 4 leaves romaine lettuce

Marinade:

- 2 teaspoons apple cider vinegar
- ¼ teaspoon smoked paprika
- 3 tablespoons maple syrup
- ¼ teaspoon onion powder
- 1 teaspoon liquid smoke
- Black pepper, to taste
- ¼ cup tamari

Directions:

1. Mix all the marinade ingredients in a bowl and add tempeh.
2. Coat it well, cover and marinate for 30 minutes. Sear the tempeh in a skillet with oil for 5 minutes per side.
3. Preheat the Breakfast Sandwich Maker until the green PREHEAT light comes on.
4. Lift cover, top rings, and cooking plates. Place a bread slice inside the bottom tray of the sandwich maker.
5. Add half of the mayo, tempeh, carrots, tomato, and lettuce. Place another bread slice on top.
6. Now lower the cooking plate and top rings. Cover the top hood, and let the sandwich cook for 5 minutes.
7. Rotate the handle of the cooking plate clockwise until it stops.
8. Lift the hood, and the rings and transfer the sandwich to a plate.
9. Repeat the same steps with the remaining ingredients.

Nutritional Value (Amount per Serving):

Calories: 284; Fat: 7.9g; Sodium: 704mg; Carbs: 38.1g; Fiber: 1.9g; Sugar: 1.9g; Protein: 14.8g

Peanut Butter Banana Bread Sandwich

Prep Time: 15 Minutes   Cook Time: 5 Minutes   Serves: 4

Preparation and Cooking Tips: You can also add a drizzle of chocolate chips to the filling.

Serving Suggestion: Would you please serve the sandwich with an apple smoothie on the side?

Ingredients:

- 8 banana bread slices, cut into 4 inches round

- 4 tablespoons chocolate-hazelnut spread
- 4 tablespoons cream cheese
- 4 tablespoons peanut butter
- 2 bananas, sliced

Directions:

1. Preheat the Breakfast Sandwich Maker until the green PREHEAT light comes on.
2. Lift cover, top rings, and cooking plates.
3. Place a bread slice, inside the bottom tray of the sandwich maker.
4. Spread ¼ of the cream cheese, chocolate spread, peanut butter, and bananas on top.
5. Now lower the cooking plate and top rings. Place the other bread slice on top.
6. Cover the top hood, and let the sandwich cook for 5 minutes.
7. Rotate the handle of the cooking plate clockwise until it stops.
8. Lift the hood, and the rings and transfer the sandwich to a plate.
9. Repeat the same steps with the remaining ingredients.

Nutritional Value (Amount per Serving):

Calories: 282; Fat: 15g; Sodium: 526mg; Carbs: 20g; Fiber: 0.6g; Sugar: 3.3g; Protein: 16g

Provolone Cheese and Portabella Mushroom Sandwich

Prep Time: 15 Minutes   Cook Time: 5 Minutes   Serves: 1

Preparation and Cooking Tips: Add some additional dried herbs to the filling.

Serving Suggestion: Serve the sandwich with crispy bacon and your favorite sauce on the side.

Ingredients:

- 1 whole wheat English muffin, sliced
- 1 portabella mushroom cap
- 1 slice provolone cheese
- 1 teaspoon olive oil
- 1 large egg, beaten
- ½ cup spring greens

Directions:

1. Preheat the Breakfast Sandwich Maker until the green PREHEAT light comes on.

2. Lift cover, top rings, and cooking plates.
3. Place the lower half of the muffin in the sandwich maker. Brush the English muffin with olive oil.
4. Put the mushroom cap on top of the English muffin.
5. Top the mushroom cap with a slice of provolone cheese.
6. Now lower the cooking plate and top rings, then pour in the egg.
7. Place greens and another muffin half on top. Cover the top hood, and let the sandwich cook for 5 minutes.
8. When finished cooking, rotate the handle of the cooking plate clockwise until it stops.
9. Lift the hood, and the rings and transfer the sandwich to a plate.

Nutritional Value (Amount per Serving):

Calories: 448; Fat: 19.3g; Sodium: 261mg; Carbs: 0.5g; Fiber: 0.3g; Sugar: 0.1g; Protein: 64.1g

Biscuit Ricotta Cheese with Nectarines

Prep Time: 15 Minutes   Cook Time: 5 Minutes   Serves: 1

Preparation and Cooking Tips: Add some additional ground black pepper to the filling.

Serving Suggestion: Serve the sandwich with your favorite sauce on the side.

Ingredients:

- 1 ripe nectarine, peeled and sliced
- 1 buttermilk biscuit, sliced
- 1 tablespoon ricotta cheese
- 1 tablespoon maple syrup
- 2 teaspoons brown sugar

Directions:

1. Preheat the Breakfast Sandwich Maker until the green PREHEAT light comes on.
2. Lift cover, top rings, and cooking plates.
3. Place the lower half of the biscuit in the sandwich maker.
4. Place the nectarines in a bowl and add the ricotta, maple syrup, and brown sugar then toss well.
5. Top the biscuit with the nectarine slices, ricotta, maple syrup, and brown sugar mixture.
6. Place the other top half of the biscuit on top of the nectarines.
7. Now lower the cooking plate and top rings. Cover

the top hood, and let the sandwich cook for 5 minutes.

8. When finished cooking, rotate the handle of the cooking plate clockwise until it stops.

9. Lift the hood, and the rings and transfer the sandwich to a plate.

Nutritional Value (Amount per Serving):

Calories: 391; Fat: 24g; Sodium: 142mg; Carbs: 38.5g; Fiber: 3.5g; Sugar: 21g; Protein: 6.6g

Mushroom and Avocado Burger

Prep Time: 15 Minutes   Cook Time: 15 Minutes   Serves: 4

Preparation and Cooking Tips: you can also add a lettuce leaf to the filling.

Serving Suggestion: Would you please serve the sandwich with crispy carrot chips on the side?

Ingredients:

- 4 Portobello mushrooms, cut in half horizontally
- 1 medium onion, cut into slices
- 1 avocado, peeled and sliced
- 4 hamburger buns, split in half
- 3 tablespoons olive oil
- ½ teaspoon black pepper
- 2 tablespoons yogurt
- ½ teaspoon garlic, minced
- 4 jarred roasted red peppers
- ¾ teaspoon salt

Directions:

1. Blend mushroom, onion, avocado, yogurt, salt, black pepper, and garlic in a food processor for 1 minute.

2. Set a suitable skillet with olive oil over medium-high heat. Make 4 equal-sized patties out of the mushroom mixture. Sear the mushroom patties in the oil for 5 minutes per side.

3. Preheat the Breakfast Sandwich Maker until the green PREHEAT light comes on. Lift cover, top rings, and cooking plates.

4. Place half of a bun, cut-side up, inside the bottom tray of the sandwich maker.

5. Lower the cooking plate and top rings then place a patty and red pepper on top.

6. Place the other half of the bun on top. Cover the top hood, and let the burger cook for 5 minutes.

7. Rotate the handle of the cooking plate clockwise

until it stops.

8. Lift the hood, and the rings and transfer the burger to a plate.

9. Repeat the same steps with the remaining ingredients.

Nutritional Value (Amount per Serving):

Calories: 282; Fat: 15g; Sodium: 526mg; Carbs: 20g; Fiber: 0.6g; Sugar: 3.3g; Protein: 16g

Dark Chocolate and Avocado Sandwich

Prep Time: 15 Minutes   Cook Time: 5 Minutes   Serves: 2

Preparation and Cooking Tips: Add some additional dried herbs to the filling.

Serving Suggestion: Serve the sandwich with your favorite sauce on the side.

Ingredients:

- 4 squares of dark chocolate, 70% cocoa, slightly crushed
- 4 slices whole-wheat bread, cut into a 4-inch circle
- ½ teaspoons light butter
- ½ cup non-fat milk
- 1 small avocado, mashed

Directions:

1. Mix avocado, milk, and chocolate bits.

2. Brush the bread slices with butter. Make two sandwiches with the avocado mix.

3. Preheat the Breakfast Sandwich Maker until the green PREHEAT light comes on.

4. Lift cover, top rings, and cooking plates. Place a sandwich in the sandwich maker.

5. Now lower the cooking plate and top rings.

6. Cover the top hood, and let the sandwich cook for 5 minutes.

7. When finished cooking, rotate the handle of the cooking plate clockwise until it stops.

8. Lift the hood, and the rings and transfer the sandwich to a plate.

9. Repeat the same steps with the remaining ingredients.

Nutritional Value (Amount per Serving):

Calories: 295; Fat: 3g; Sodium: 355mg; Carbs: 10g; Fiber: 1g; Sugar: 5g; Protein: 1g

Cheddar and Apple Cinnamon Raisin Sandwich

Prep Time: 15 Minutes   Cook Time: 5 Minutes   Serves: 1

Preparation and Cooking Tips: Add some additional ground black pepper to the filling.

Serving Suggestion: Serve the sandwich with your favorite sauce on the side.

Ingredients:

- 2 slices cinnamon raisin bread, cut into 4-inch circle
- Pinch ground cinnamon and nutmeg
- ½ small apple, sliced thin
- 1 thin slice cheddar cheese
- ½ teaspoon unsalted butter

Directions:

1. Preheat the Breakfast Sandwich Maker until the green PREHEAT light comes on.
2. Lift cover, top rings, and cooking plates. Place the lower half of the muffin in the sandwich maker.
3. Place one slice of bread inside the bottom tray of the sandwich maker.
4. Spread the bread with butter. Now lower the cooking plate and top rings.
5. Top with the slices of apple, then sprinkle them with cinnamon and nutmeg.
6. Place the slice of cheddar cheese over the apples.
7. Top the cheese with the other piece of bread. Cover the top hood, and let the sandwich cook for 5 minutes.
8. When finished cooking, rotate the handle of the cooking plate clockwise until it stops.
9. Lift the hood, and the rings and transfer the sandwich to a plate.

Nutritional Value (Amount per Serving):

Calories: 432; Fat: 9.5g; Sodium: 515.8mg; Carbs: 33.2g; Fiber: 0.2g; Sugar: 0.1g; Protein: 9.4g

Honey Nut Mix Sandwich

Prep Time: 15 Minutes   Cook Time: 5 Minutes   Serves: 2

Preparation and Cooking Tips: You can also add a drizzle of paprika on top of the filling.

Serving Suggestion: Serve the sandwich with coleslaw and your favorite sauce on the side.

Ingredients:

- ¼ cup roasted mixed nuts (almonds, walnuts, cashews, pecans, etc.)
- 4 slices whole-wheat bread, cut into a 4-inch circle
- ½ teaspoons light butter
- 1 tablespoon wild honey

Directions:

1. Mix the mixed nuts and honey.
2. Make two sandwiches with the honeyed mixed nuts.
3. Preheat the Breakfast Sandwich Maker until the green PREHEAT light comes on.
4. Lift cover, top rings, and cooking plates. Lightly pat butter on each sandwich maker pan.
5. Place one sandwich in the sandwich maker. Now lower the cooking plate and top.
6. Cover the top hood, and let the sandwich cook for 5 minutes.
7. When finished cooking, rotate the handle of the cooking plate clockwise until it stops.
8. Lift the hood, and the rings and transfer the sandwich to a plate.
9. Repeat the same steps with the remaining ingredients.

Nutritional Value (Amount per Serving):

Calories: 173; Fat: 9.8g; Sodium: 112.2mg; Carbs: 17.5g; Fiber: 1.2g; Sugar: 12.2g; Protein: 3.9g

Egg Whites and Cheese Ciabatta

Prep Time: 15 Minutes   Cook Time: 5 Minutes   Serves: 1

Preparation and Cooking Tips: Add some additional ground black pepper to the filling.

Serving Suggestion: Serve the sandwich with coleslaw and your favorite sauce on the side.

Ingredients:

- ⅛ teaspoon dried Italian seasoning
- 1 ciabatta sandwich bun, sliced
- 1 teaspoon chopped chives
- 1 teaspoon unsalted butter
- 1 slice of mozzarella cheese
- 2 large egg whites
- 1 tablespoon skim milk
- 1 garlic clove, minced

Directions:

1. Preheat the Breakfast Sandwich Maker until the

green PREHEAT light comes on.

2. Lift cover, top rings, and cooking plates. Place the lower half of the bun in the sandwich maker.
3. Spread the butter on the ciabatta bun. Top with a slice of mozzarella cheese.
4. Whisk together the egg whites, milk, garlic, chives, and Italian seasoning.
5. Now lower the cooking plate and top rings, then pour in the egg.
6. Place the other half of the bun on top.
7. Cover the top hood, and let the sandwich cook for 5 minutes.
8. When finished cooking, rotate the handle of the cooking plate clockwise until it stops.
9. Lift the hood, and the rings and transfer the sandwich to a plate.

Nutritional Value (Amount per Serving):

Calories: 545; Fat: 36g; Sodium: 272mg; Carbs: 41g; Fiber: 0.2g; Sugar: 0.1g; Protein: 42.5g

Pineapple, Apple, and Banana Sandwich

Prep Time: 15 Minutes   Cook Time: 5 Minutes   Serves: 2

Preparation and Cooking Tips: You can also add a drizzle of sprinkles to the filling.

Serving Suggestion: Serve the sandwich with an avocado smoothie on the side.

Ingredients:

- 4 whole wheat brown bread, cut into 4 inches round
- 2 ripe bananas, peeled and sliced
- 2 tablespoons mixed fruit jam
- 2 pineapples, sliced thin
- 1 apple, sliced

Directions:

1. Preheat the Breakfast Sandwich Maker until the green PREHEAT light comes on.
2. Lift cover, top rings, and cooking plates.
3. Place a bread slice, inside the bottom tray of the sandwich maker.
4. Spread ½ of the jam, apple, pineapple and bananas.
5. Place the other bread slice on top. Now lower the cooking plate and top rings then.
6. Cover the top hood, and let the sandwich cook for 5 minutes.
7. Rotate the handle of the cooking plate clockwise

until it stops.
8. Lift the hood, and the rings and transfer the sandwich to a plate.
9. Repeat the same steps with the remaining ingredients.

Nutritional Value (Amount per Serving):

Calories: 282; Fat: 15g; Sodium: 526mg; Carbs: 20g; Fiber: 0.6g; Sugar: 3.3g; Protein: 16g

Honey Pear and Blueberry Croissant

Prep Time: 15 Minutes   Cook Time: 5 Minutes   Serves: 2

Preparation and Cooking Tips: You can also add lettuce leaves to the filling.

Serving Suggestion: Serve the sandwich with crispy bacon and your favorite sauce on the side.

Ingredients:

- 3 tablespoons of cream cheese, brought to room temperature
- 1 large pear (bosc pears are a perfect choice), sliced
- ½ cup of blueberries, rinsed, drained and dried
- 2 medium croissants, sliced in half
- 2 tablespoons of honey

Directions:

1. Preheat the Breakfast Sandwich Maker until the green PREHEAT light comes on. Lift cover, top rings, and cooking plates.
2. Take 1½ teaspoons of the cream cheese, spreading half of it on the top of the croissant and half on the croissant's bottom.
3. Place the croissant bottom in the bottom slot of the sandwich maker, topped with half of the pear slices.
4. Add ¼ cup of blueberries on top of the pear slices. Take a tablespoon of the honey, drizzling it carefully over the fruit.
5. Lower the cooking plate and top rings, then place the other half of the croissant on top.
6. Cover the top hood, and let the sandwich cook for 5 minutes.
7. When finished cooking, rotate the handle of the cooking plate clockwise until it stops.
8. Lift the hood, and the rings and transfer the sandwich to a plate.
9. Repeat the same steps with the remaining ingredients.

Nutritional Value (Amount per Serving):

Calories: 245; Fat: 14g; Sodium: 122mg; Carbs: 23.3g; Fiber: 1.2g; Sugar: 12g; Protein: 4.3g

Peanut Butter and Banana Sandwich

Prep Time: 15 Minutes   Cook Time: 5 Minutes   Serves: 2

Preparation and Cooking Tips. Add some additional ground black pepper to the filling.

Serving Suggestion: Serve the sandwich with your favorite sauce on the side.

Ingredients:

- 4 slices whole-wheat bread, cut into a 4-inch circle
- 1 medium banana, slightly crushed
- ½ teaspoons light butter
- 1 tablespoon peanut butter

Directions:

1. Make two sandwiches, layering peanut butter spread and crushed bananas.
2. Preheat the Breakfast Sandwich Maker until the green PREHEAT light comes on.
3. Lift cover, top rings, and cooking plates. Lightly pat butter on each sandwich maker pan.
4. Place a sandwich in the sandwich maker.
5. Now lower the cooking plate and top rings.
6. Cover the top hood, and let the sandwich cook for 5 minutes.
7. When finished cooking, rotate the handle of the cooking plate clockwise until it stops.
8. Lift the hood, and the rings and transfer the sandwich to a plate.
9. Repeat the same steps with the remaining ingredients.

Nutritional Value (Amount per Serving):

Calories: 121; Fat: 7.1g; Sodium: 110mg; Carbs: 5g; Fiber: 0.5g; Sugar: 1.1g; Protein: 10 g

Garlicky Tofu Burgers

Prep Time: 15 Minutes   Cook Time: 15 Minutes   Serves: 6

Preparation and Cooking Tips: Add a layer of pickled veggies for a change of taste.

Serving Suggestion: Would you please serve the sandwich with crispy fries on the side?

Ingredients:

Burgers:
- ½ (14-ounces) extra-firm tofu, drained
- 2 tablespoons wheat germ
- 2 tablespoons all-purpose flour
- 2 tablespoons garlic powder
- 1 tablespoon oil for frying
- 2 tablespoons soy sauce • 3 green onions, diced
- 1 medium onion, diced   • Dash of pepper

Serving:
- 6 hamburger buns
- 6 lettuce leaves
- 6 slices tomato

Directions:

1. Blend tofu with onion, wheat germ, flour, garlic powder, soy sauce, green onions, and black pepper in a food processor for 1 minute.
2. Set a suitable skillet with olive oil over medium-high heat. Make 6 equal-sized patties out of the turkey mixture. Sear the tofu patties in the oil for 5 minutes per side.
3. Preheat the Breakfast Sandwich Maker until the green PREHEAT light comes on. Lift cover, top rings, and cooking plates.
4. Place half of a bun, cut-side up, inside the bottom tray of the sandwich maker.
5. Lower the cooking plate and top rings then place a patty, a lettuce leaf, and a tomato slice on top.
6. Place the other half of the bun on top. Cover the top hood, and let the burger cook for 5 minutes.
7. Rotate the handle of the cooking plate clockwise until it stops.
8. Lift the hood, and the rings and transfer the burger to a plate.
9. Repeat the same steps with the remaining ingredients.

Nutritional Value (Amount per Serving):

Calories: 180; Fat: 3.2g; Sodium: 133mg; Carbs: 32g; Fiber: 1.1g; Sugar: 1.8g; Protein: 9g

Cheese and Avocado Nutella Sandwich

Prep Time: 15 Minutes   Cook Time: 5 Minutes   Serves: 2

Preparation and Cooking Tips: You can also add a drizzle

of chocolate chips to the filling.

Serving Suggestion: Would you please serve the sandwich with a glass of chocolate smoothie on the side?

Ingredients:

- 4 whole-wheat bread slices, cut into 4 inches round
- 2 tablespoon Nutella spread
- 2 tablespoons cream cheese
- 1 avocado, sliced

Directions:

1. Preheat the Breakfast Sandwich Maker until the green PREHEAT light comes on.
2. Lift cover, top rings, and cooking plates.
3. Place a bread slice, inside the bottom tray of the sandwich maker.
4. Spread ½ of the cream cheese, Nutella, and avocado on top.
5. Place the other bread slice on top. Now lower the cooking plate and top rings then.
6. Cover the top hood, and let the sandwich cook for 5 minutes.
7. Rotate the handle of the cooking plate clockwise until it stops.
8. Lift the hood, and the rings and transfer the sandwich to a plate.
9. Repeat the same steps with the remaining ingredients.

Nutritional Value (Amount per Serving):

Calories: 282; Fat: 15g; Sodium: 526mg; Carbs: 20g; Fiber: 0.6g; Sugar: 3.3g; Protein: 16g

Garlic Buffalo Chickpeas Burgers

Prep Time: 15 Minutes   Cook Time: 12 Minutes   Serves: 4

Preparation and Cooking Tips: Add a layer of spicy mayo and pickled veggies for a change of taste.

Serving Suggestion: Would you please serve the sandwich with crispy fries on the side?

Ingredients:

- 1½ cups canned chickpeas, drained
- 3 tablespoons Frank's red hot sauce
- 1 tablespoon non-dairy butter
- ¼ teaspoon granulated onion
- 4 hamburger buns, split in half
- 1 teaspoon canola oil
- ¼ cup chopped onion
- 1 garlic clove minced

Directions:

1. Sauté chickpeas with oil, onion, garlic, red hot sauce, onion, and butter in a skillet for 7 minutes.
2. Preheat the Breakfast Sandwich Maker until the green PREHEAT light comes on.
3. Lift cover, top rings, and cooking plates.
4. Place half of a bun, cut-side up, inside the bottom tray of the sandwich maker.
5. Spread ¼ of the chickpeas over the bun. Now lower the cooking plate and top rings.
6. Place the other half of the muffin on top. Cover the top hood, and let the burger cook for 5 minutes.
7. Rotate the handle of the cooking plate clockwise until it stops.
8. Lift the hood, and the rings and transfer the burger to a plate.
9. Repeat the same steps with the remaining ingredients.

Nutritional Value (Amount per Serving):

Calories: 282; Fat: 15g; Sodium: 526mg; Carbs: 20g; Fiber: 0.6g; Sugar: 3.3g; Protein: 16g

Brie and Apricot Croissant with Pecans

Prep Time: 15 Minutes   Cook Time: 5 Minutes   Serves: 1

Preparation and Cooking Tips: You can also add lettuce leaves to the filling.

Serving Suggestion: Serve the sandwich with coleslaw and your favorite sauce on the side.

Ingredients:

- 1 ounce of brie, cut into slices, rind removed
- ½ tablespoon of chopped, glazed pecans
- 1 tablespoon of apricot preserves
- ½ teaspoon of dark brown sugar
- 1 medium croissant
- Cinnamon to taste

Directions:

1. Preheat the Breakfast Sandwich Maker until the green PREHEAT light comes on.
2. Lift cover, top rings, and cooking plates.
3. Place the lower half of the croissant in the sandwich

maker.

4. Now lower the cooking plate and top rings and place the cheese on top.

5. Spread the apricot preserves on top of the cheese. Sprinkle with cinnamon, pecans, and sugar on top.

6. Place the other top half of the croissant on top.

7. Cover the top hood, and let the sandwich cook for 5 minutes.

8. When finished cooking, rotate the handle of the cooking plate clockwise until it stops.

9. Lift the hood, and the rings and transfer the sandwich to a plate.

Nutritional Value (Amount per Serving):

Calories: 273; Fat: 9.4g; Sodium: 140mg; Carbs: 47.2g; Fiber: 1.9g; Sugar: 30.4g; Protein: 2.7g

Chapter 8: Snacks and Desserts Sandwich

Strawberry Cinnamon English Muffin Pies

Prep Time: 15 Minutes   Cook Time: 12 Minutes   Serves: 6

Preparation and Cooking Tips: you can also add some mascarpone to the filling.

Serving Suggestion: Serve the pie with an apple smoothie on the side.

Ingredients:

- 6 English muffins, cut in half
- 3 tablespoons cornstarch
- ½ teaspoon ground cinnamon
- 1 tablespoon fresh lemon juice
- 2½ cups fresh strawberries
- 1 teaspoon lemon zest
- ½ cup sugar
- 2 tablespoons of water
- A pinch of salt
- Sugar, for sprinkling
- 1 egg yolk

Directions:

1. Mix strawberries with lemon juice, zest, cinnamon, salt, sugar, and cornstarch in a saucepan.
2. Stir and cook berries on low heat for 7 minutes. Allow this berry filling to cool at room temperature.
3. Preheat the Breakfast Sandwich Maker until the green PREHEAT light comes on.
4. Lift cover, top rings, and cooking plates. Place half of a muffin inside the bottom tray of the sandwich maker.
5. Add a tablespoon of berry filing to its center. Place the other half of the muffin on top.
6. Now lower the cooking plate and top rings. Cover the top hood, and let the sandwich cook for 5 minutes.
7. Rotate the handle of the cooking plate clockwise until it stops.
8. Lift the hood, and the rings and transfer the sandwich to a plate.
9. Make more berry pies in the same way.

Nutritional Value (Amount per Serving):

Calories: 351; Fat: 19g; Sodium: 412mg; Carbs: 13g; Fiber: 0.3g; Sugar: 1g; Protein: 23g

Apple, Ham, and Cheese Panini

Prep Time: 15 Minutes   Cook Time: 5 Minutes   Serves: 4

Preparation and Cooking Tips: Add some additional ground black pepper to the filling.

Serving Suggestion: Serve the sandwich with crispy bacon and your favorite sauce on the side.

Ingredients:

- 8 slices multigrain bread, cut into a 4-inch circle
- 1 small apple cored and thinly sliced
- 2 tablespoons mayonnaise
- 2 tablespoons Dijon mustard
- 4 tablespoons butter softened
- 8 ounces thick-sliced ham pieces
- 8-ounce Swiss cheese grated

Directions:

1. Preheat the Breakfast Sandwich Maker until the green PREHEAT light comes on.
2. Lift cover, top rings, and cooking plates.
3. Place a bread slice in the sandwich maker and top with ¼ th of the mayo, mustard, and butter.
4. Lower the cooking plate and top rings, then add ¼ th of the apple, ham, and cheese.
5. Add the other circle of the bread on top.
6. Cover the top hood, and let the sandwich cook for 5 minutes.
7. When finished cooking, rotate the handle of the cooking plate clockwise until it stops.
8. Lift the hood, and the rings and transfer the sandwich to a plate.
9. Repeat the same steps with the remaining ingredients.

Nutritional Value (Amount per Serving):

Calories: 229; Fat: 1.9; Sodium: 567mg; Carbs: 1.9g; Fiber: 0.4g; Sugar: 0.6g; Protein: 11.8g

Ganache Raspberry Paninis

Prep Time: 15 Minutes   Cook Time: 5 Minutes   Serves: 2

Preparation and Cooking Tips: Add some additional dried herbs to the filling.

Serving Suggestion: Serve the sandwich with your favorite sauce on the side.

Ingredients:

- 4 slices Panera Bread, cut into a 4-inch circle
- 4-ounce cream cheese softened
- 4 tablespoons raspberry jam
- ½ cup chocolate ganache

Directions:

1. Preheat the Breakfast Sandwich Maker until the green PREHEAT light comes on.
2. Lift cover, top rings, and cooking plates.
3. Place one circle of the bread in the sandwich maker.
4. Top it with ½ of the chocolate ganache, jam, and cream cheese.
5. Now lower the cooking plate and top rings. Add the other circle of the bread on top.
6. Cover the top hood, and let the sandwich cook for 5 minutes.
7. When finished cooking, rotate the handle of the cooking plate clockwise until it stops.
8. Lift the hood, and the rings and transfer the sandwich to a plate.
9. Repeat the same steps with the remaining ingredients.

Nutritional Value (Amount per Serving):

Calories: 245; Fat: 14g; Sodium: 122mg; Carbs: 23.3g; Fiber: 1.2g; Sugar: 12g; Protein: 4.3g

Lemony Raspberry English Muffin Pies

Prep Time: 15 Minutes   Cook Time: 12 Minutes   Serves: 6

Preparation and Cooking Tips: you can also add some extra cream to the filling.
Serving Suggestion: Would you please serve the pie with a banana smoothie on the side?

Ingredients:

- ½ teaspoon ground cinnamon
- 1 tablespoon fresh lemon juice
- 2½ cups fresh raspberries
- 3 tablespoons cornstarch • ½ cup sugar
- 2 tablespoons of water   • 6 English muffin
- Sugar, for sprinkling   • A pinch of salt
- 1 teaspoon lemon zest   • 1 egg yolk

Directions:

1. Mix raspberries with lemon juice, zest, cinnamon, salt, sugar, and cornstarch in a saucepan.
2. Stir and cook berries on low heat for 7 minutes. Allow this berry filling to cool at room temperature.
3. Preheat the Breakfast Sandwich Maker until the green PREHEAT light comes on.
4. Lift cover, top rings, and cooking plates. Place half of a muffin inside the bottom tray of the sandwich maker.

5. Add a tablespoon of berry filing to its center. Place the other half of the muffin on top.
6. Now lower the cooking plate and top rings. Cover the top hood, and let the sandwich cook for 5 minutes.
7. Rotate the handle of the cooking plate clockwise until it stops.
8. Lift the hood, and the rings and transfer the sandwich to a plate.
9. Make more berry pies in the same way.

Nutritional Value (Amount per Serving):

Calories: 351; Fat: 19g; Sodium: 412mg; Carbs: 13g; Fiber: 0.3g; Sugar: 1g; Protein: 23g

Cheese and Raspberry Sandwiches

Prep Time: 15 Minutes   Cook Time: 5 Minutes   Serves: 2

Preparation and Cooking Tips: you can also add some heavy cream to the filling.
Serving Suggestion: Would you please serve the sandwich with a strawberry smoothie on the side?

Ingredients:

- 12 ounces of semi-sweet chocolate
- 12 ounces fresh raspberries
- 2 English muffins split in half • 8 ounces brie cheese

Directions:

1. Preheat the Breakfast Sandwich Maker until the green PREHEAT light comes on.
2. Lift cover, top rings, and cooking plates.
3. Place half of the English muffin, cut-side up, inside the bottom tray of the sandwich maker.
4. Spread half of the fillings and place the other muffin half on top.
5. Now lower the cooking plate and top rings.
6. Cover the top hood, and let the sandwich cook for 5 minutes.
7. Rotate the handle of the cooking plate clockwise until it stops.
8. Lift the hood, and the rings and transfer the sandwich to a plate.
9. Repeat the same steps with the remaining ingredients.

Nutritional Value (Amount per Serving):

Calories: 338; Fat: 7g; Sodium: 316mg; Carbs: 24g; Fiber: 0.3g; Sugar: 0.3g; Protein: 3g

Guacamole Chicken and Tomato Panini

Prep Time: 15 Minutes   Cook Time: 5 Minutes   Serves: 1

Preparation and Cooking Tips: Add some additional dried herbs to the filling.

Serving Suggestion: Serve the sandwich with your favorite sauce on the side.

Ingredients:

- 2 slices or a sprinkle of vegan cheese or cheese of choice
- 2 slices gluten-free bread, cut into a 4-inch circle
- 4 ounces grilled chicken breast
- ½ avocado mashed
- Salt and black pepper
- 3 slices of tomato

Directions:

1. Preheat the Breakfast Sandwich Maker until the green PREHEAT light comes on.
2. Lift cover, top rings, and cooking plates.
3. Place a bread slice in the sandwich maker.
4. Now lower the cooking plate and top rings, then add chicken and the rest of the ingredients on top.
5. Add the other circle of the bread on top.
6. Cover the top hood, and let the sandwich cook for 5 minutes.
7. When finished cooking, rotate the handle of the cooking plate clockwise until it stops.
8. Lift the hood, and the rings and transfer the sandwich to a plate.

Nutritional Value (Amount per Serving):

C Calories: 122; Fat: 1.8g; Sodium: 794mg; Carbs: 17g; Fiber: 8.9g; Sugar: 1.6g; Protein: 14.9g

Brie Chocolate Panini

Prep Time: 15 Minutes   Cook Time: 5 Minutes   Serves: 2

Preparation and Cooking Tips: You can also add lettuce leaves to the filling.

Serving Suggestion: Serve the sandwich with your favorite sauce on the side.

Ingredients:

- 4 slices crunchy sourdough bread, cut into 4-inch circle
- 2 Tablespoons unsalted butter, melted
- 4 ounces Brie cheese, cut into slices

- 2-ounces milk chocolate

Directions:

1. Preheat the Breakfast Sandwich Maker until the green PREHEAT light comes on.
2. Lift cover, top rings, and cooking plates.
3. Place one bread slice in the sandwich maker and top it with ½ of the butter, brie, and chocolate.
4. Now lower the cooking plate and top rings.
5. Add the other circle of the bread on top.
6. Cover the top hood, and let the sandwich cook for 5 minutes.
7. When finished cooking, rotate the handle of the cooking plate clockwise until it stops.
8. Lift the hood, and the rings and transfer the sandwich to a plate.
9. Repeat the same steps with the remaining ingredients.

Nutritional Value (Amount per Serving):

Calories: 209; Fat: 7.5g; Sodium: 321mg; Carbs: 34.1g; Fiber: 4g; Sugar: 3.8g; Protein: 4.3g

Chocolate Pumpkin Brie Sandwich

Prep Time: 15 Minutes   Cook Time: 5 Minutes   Serves: 1

Preparation and Cooking Tips: you can also add some mascarpone to the filling.

Serving Suggestion: Serve the sandwich with an avocado smoothie on the side.

Ingredients:

- 2 slices of French bread, cut into 4 inches round
- 1½ ounces of chocolate broken into pieces
- 1 tablespoon butter softened
- 2 ounces of brie cheese sliced
- ¼ cup pumpkin butter

Directions:

1. Preheat the Breakfast Sandwich Maker until the green PREHEAT light comes on.
2. Lift cover, top rings, and cooking plates.
3. Place a bread slice inside the bottom tray of the sandwich maker.
4. Spread butter, pumpkin butter, brie cheese, and chocolate on top.
5. Now lower the cooking plate and top rings.
6. Place another bread slice on top.

7. Cover the top hood, and let the sandwich cook for 5 minutes.
8. Rotate the handle of the cooking plate clockwise until it stops.
9. Lift the hood, and the rings and transfer the sandwich to a plate.

Nutritional Value (Amount per Serving):

Calories: 301; Fat: 5g; Sodium: 340mg; Carbs: 17g; Fiber: 1.2g; Sugar: 1.3g; Protein: 15.3g

Chocolate Dessert Panini

Prep Time: 15 Minutes   Cook Time: 5 Minutes   Serves: 1

Preparation and Cooking Tips: Add some additional ground black pepper to the filling.

Serving Suggestion: Serve the sandwich with crispy bacon and your favorite sauce on the side.

Ingredients:

- 2 white bread slices, cut into 4-inch circle
- 1 jumbo marshmallow toasted
- 2 tablespoons chocolate

Directions:

1. Preheat the Breakfast Sandwich Maker until the green PREHEAT light comes on.
2. Lift cover, top rings, and cooking plates.
3. Place one circle of the bread in the sandwich maker.
4. Top it with Hershey's chocolate spread.
5. Lower the cooking plate and top rings, then spread marshmallows on top.
6. Add the other circle of the bread on top.
7. Cover the top hood, and let the sandwich cook for 5 minutes.
8. When finished cooking, rotate the handle of the cooking plate clockwise until it stops.
9. Lift the hood, and the rings and transfer the sandwich to a plate.

Nutritional Value (Amount per Serving):

Calories: 198; Fat: 14g; Sodium: 272mg; Carbs: 34g; Fiber: 1g; Sugar: 9.3g; Protein: 1.3g

Mini Vanilla Cake

Prep Time: 15 Minutes   Cook Time: 5 Minutes   Serves: 1

Preparation and Cooking Tips: You can also add a drizzle of lemon juice on top of the filling.

Serving Suggestion: Serve the sandwich with coleslaw and your favorite sauce on the side.

Ingredients:

- ½ cup all-purpose flour/ maida
- ½ teaspoon baking powder
- ½ teaspoon vanilla essence
- ¼ cup cooking oil/butter   • 2 tablespoons milk
- 3 tablespoons sugar   • 1 egg

Directions:

1. Add egg and sugar in a bowl and whisk until the mixture changes color and fluffs up.
2. Now add milk, vanilla essence, and oil to the egg mixture and whisk again to combine everything.
3. Add in all-purpose flour, and baking powder and fold everything well with a spatula.
4. Preheat the Breakfast Sandwich Maker until the green PREHEAT light comes on.
5. Lift cover, top rings, and cooking plates.
6. Lower the cooking plate and top rings then pour in the prepared batter.
7. Cover the top hood, and let the sandwich cook for 5 minutes.
8. When finished cooking, rotate the handle of the cooking plate clockwise until it stops.
9. Lift the hood, and the rings and transfer the sandwich to a plate.

Nutritional Value (Amount per Serving):

Calories: 192; Fat: 9.3g; Sodium: 133mg; Carbs: 27.1g; Fiber: 1.4g; Sugar: 19g; Protein: 3.2g

Chocolate Marshmallow Banana Sandwiches

Prep Time: 15 Minutes   Cook Time: 5 Minutes   Serves: 2

Preparation and Cooking Tips: you can also add some whipped cream to the filling.

Serving Suggestion: Would you please serve the sandwich with a mango smoothie on the side?

Ingredients:

- 4 slices buttermilk bread, cut into 4 inches round
- 2 tablespoons semisweet chocolate chips
- 2 tablespoons unsalted butter
- 2 tablespoons dark brown sugar
- 8 whole large marshmallows
- 12 banana slices

Directions:

1. Preheat the Breakfast Sandwich Maker until the green PREHEAT light comes on.
2. Lift cover, top rings, and cooking plates.
3. Place a bread slice inside the bottom tray of the sandwich maker.
4. Spread ½ of the butter, sugar, chocolate chips, banana slices, and marshmallows.
5. Now lower the cooking plate and top rings. Place another bread slice on top.
6. Cover the top hood, and let the sandwich cook for 5 minutes.
7. Rotate the handle of the cooking plate clockwise until it stops.
8. Lift the hood, and the rings and transfer the sandwich to a plate.
9. Repeat the same steps with the remaining ingredients.

Nutritional Value (Amount per Serving):

Calories: 110; Fat: 6g; Sodium: 220mg; Carbs: 32g; Fiber: 2.4g; Sugar: 1.2g; Protein: 12g

Nut Butter Banana Chocolate Chip

Prep Time: 15 Minutes   Cook Time: 5 Minutes   Serves: 1

Preparation and Cooking Tips: You can also add a drizzle of paprika on top of the filling.
Serving Suggestion: Serve the sandwich with coleslaw and your favorite sauce on the side.

Ingredients:

- 2 tablespoons natural peanut or almond butter (no added salt or sugar)
- 2 slices whole-grain bread, cut into a 4-inch circle
- 10 bittersweet chocolate chips (60% cocoa)
- ½ banana, sliced

Directions:

1. Preheat the Breakfast Sandwich Maker until the green PREHEAT light comes on.
2. Lift cover, top rings, and cooking plates.
3. Place one bread slice in the sandwich maker and top it with peanut butter and chocolate chips.
4. Lower the cooking plate and top rings, then add the banana.
5. Add the other circle of the bread on top.
6. Cover the top hood, and let the sandwich cook for 5 minutes.

7. When finished cooking, rotate the handle of the cooking plate clockwise until it stops.
8. Lift the hood, and the rings and transfer the sandwich to a plate.

Nutritional Value (Amount per Serving):

Calories: 267; Fat: 12g; Sodium: 165mg; Carbs: 39g; Fiber: 1.4g; Sugar: 22g; Protein: 3.3g

Cinnamon Buttery Nutella Quesadilla

Prep Time: 15 Minutes   Cook Time: 5 Minutes   Serves: 1

Preparation and Cooking Tips: you can add some crushed crackers to the filling as well.
Serving Suggestion: Serve the quesadilla with a banana smoothie on the side.

Ingredients:

- 1 (10 inches) flour tortilla, cut into two 4 inches rounds
- ¼ cup granulated sugar   • 1 tablespoon butter
- 1 tablespoon cinnamon   • 2-3 tablespoons Nutella

Directions:

1. Preheat the Breakfast Sandwich Maker until the green PREHEAT light comes on.
2. Lift cover, top rings, and cooking plates.
3. Place a tortilla round inside the bottom tray of the sandwich maker.
4. Spread Nutella, cinnamon, sugar, and butter on top.
5. Now lower the cooking plate and top rings.
6. Place a tortilla round on top.
7. Cover the top hood, and let the sandwich cook for 5 minutes.
8. Rotate the handle of the cooking plate clockwise until it stops.
9. Lift the hood, and the rings and transfer the sandwich to a plate.

Nutritional Value (Amount per Serving):

Calories: 256; Fat: 4g; Sodium: 634mg; Carbs: 33g; Fiber: 1.4g; Sugar: 1g; Protein: 3g

Buttery Chocolate Raspberry Sandwiches

Prep Time: 15 Minutes   Cook Time: 5 Minutes   Serves: 4

Preparation and Cooking Tips: you can also add sprinkles

to the filling.

Serving Suggestion: Would you please serve the sandwich with a banana smoothie on the side?

Ingredients:

- 8 (¼-inch) slices Portuguese, cut into 4 inches rounds
- 12 (53-ounce) packages dark chocolate squares
- ¼ cup seedless raspberry preserves
- 8 teaspoons butter   • Coarse sea salt

Directions:

1. Preheat the Breakfast Sandwich Maker until the green PREHEAT light comes on.
2. Lift cover, top rings, and cooking plates.
3. Place a bread slice, inside the bottom tray of the sandwich maker.
4. Spread ¼ of the raspberry preserves, chocolate squares, and butter on top.
5. Now lower the cooking plate and top rings. Place another bread slice on top.
6. Cover the top hood, and let the sandwich cook for 5 minutes.
7. Rotate the handle of the cooking plate clockwise until it stops.
8. Lift the hood, and the rings and transfer the sandwich to a plate.
9. Repeat the same steps with the remaining ingredients.

Nutritional Value (Amount per Serving):

Calories: 293; Fat: 3g; Sodium: 510mg; Carbs: 12g; Fiber: 3g; Sugar: 4g; Protein: 4g

Chocolate Pomegranate Sandwich

Prep Time: 15 Minutes   Cook Time: 5 Minutes   Serves: 2

Preparation and Cooking Tips: you can also add whipped cream to the filling.

Serving Suggestion: Would you please serve the sandwich with a chocolate smoothie on the side?

Ingredients:

- 4 slices whole-grain crusty bread, cut into 4 inches round
- 3 tablespoons pomegranate perils
- 2 mini squares of dark chocolate
- 2 tablespoons dairy-free butter

- 4 tablespoons almond butter

Directions:

1. Preheat the Breakfast Sandwich Maker until the green PREHEAT light comes on.
2. Lift cover, top rings, and cooking plates.
3. Place a bread slice inside the bottom tray of the sandwich maker.
4. Spread ½ of the butter, almond butter, chocolate and pomegranate perils.
5. Now lower the cooking plate and top rings. Place a bread slice on top.
6. Cover the top hood, and let the sandwich cook for 5 minutes.
7. Rotate the handle of the cooking plate clockwise until it stops.
8. Lift the hood, and the rings and transfer the sandwich to a plate.
9. Repeat the same steps with the remaining ingredients.

Nutritional Value (Amount per Serving):

Calories: 248; Fat: 23g; Sodium: 350mg; Carbs: 18g; Fiber: 6.3g; Sugar: 1g; Protein: 40.3g

Avocado, Tomato, and Spinach Panini

Prep Time: 15 Minutes   Cook Time: 5 Minutes   Serves: 1

Preparation and Cooking Tips: Add some additional dried herbs to the filling.

Serving Suggestion: Serve the sandwich with your favorite sauce on the side.

Ingredients:

- 2 sourdough bread slices, cut into 4-inch circle
- 1 slice Colby jack cheese • 6 leaves of spinach
- 1 tablespoon light mayo • 2 slices tomatoes
- 1 tablespoon butter   • ½ avocado sliced

Directions:

1. Preheat the Breakfast Sandwich Maker until the green PREHEAT light comes on.
2. Lift cover, top rings, and cooking plates.
3. Place one bread slice in the sandwich maker and top it with mayo, butter, and spinach.
4. Now lower the cooking plate and top rings, then add avocado, tomato, and cheese.
5. Add the other circle of the bread on top.

6. Cover the top hood, and let the sandwich cook for 5 minutes.
7. When finished cooking, rotate the handle of the cooking plate clockwise until it stops.
8. Lift the hood, and the rings and transfer the sandwich to a plate.

Nutritional Value (Amount per Serving):

Calories: 237; Fat: 19g; Sodium: 518mg; Carbs: 7g; Fiber: 1.5g, Sugar: 3.4g; Protein: 12g

Balsamic Caprese Panini

Prep Time: 15 Minutes   Cook Time: 5 Minutes   Serves: 1

Preparation and Cooking Tips: You can also add a layer of your favorite sauce to the filling.

Serving Suggestion: Serve the sandwich with coleslaw and your favorite sauce on the side.

Ingredients:

- 2 sourdough bread slices, cut into 4-inch circle
- 1 teaspoon balsamic vinegar
- 2 slices fresh mozzarella • ½ Mato sliced
- Handful of basil leaves   • Salt and black pepper
- 2 tablespoons olive oil

Directions:

1. Preheat the Breakfast Sandwich Maker until the green PREHEAT light comes on.
2. Lift cover, top rings, and cooking plates.
3. Place a bread slice in the sandwich maker.
4. Lower the cooking plate and top rings then add Mato and the rest of the fillings.
5. Add the other circle of the bread on top.
6. Cover the top hood, and let the sandwich cook for 5 minutes.
7. When finished cooking, rotate the handle of the cooking plate clockwise until it stops.
8. Lift the hood, and the rings and transfer the sandwich to a plate.

Nutritional Value (Amount per Serving):

Calories: 307; Fat: 8.6g; Sodium: 510mg; Carbs: 22.2g; Fiber: 1.4g; Sugar: 13g; Protein: 33.6g

Banana Nutella Panini

Prep Time: 15 Minutes   Cook Time: 5 Minutes   Serves: 2

Preparation and Cooking Tips: Add some additional dried herbs to the filling.

Serving Suggestion: Serve the sandwich with crispy bacon and your favorite sauce on the side.

Ingredients:

- 4 slices French bread, cut into 4-inch circles
- 6 tablespoons Marshmallow cream
- 6 tablespoons Nutella spread
- 1 large banana sliced   • 2-3 tablespoons butter

Directions:

1. Preheat the Breakfast Sandwich Maker until the green PREHEAT light comes on.
2. Lift cover, top rings, and cooking plates.
3. Place one bread slice in the sandwich maker and top it with ½ of butter, spread, and cream.
4. Lower the cooking plate and top rings then add ½ of the banana.
5. Add the other circle of the bread on top.
6. Cover the top hood, and let the sandwich cook for 5 minutes.
7. When finished cooking, rotate the handle of the cooking plate clockwise until it stops.
8. Lift the hood, and the rings and transfer the sandwich to a plate.
9. Repeat the same steps with the remaining ingredients.

Nutritional Value (Amount per Serving):

Calories: 190; Fat: 18g; Sodium: 150mg; Carbs: 0.6g; Fiber: 0.4g; Sugar: 0.4g; Protein: 7.2g

Kanafeh Sandwich with Pistachios

Prep Time: 15 Minutes   Cook Time: 12 Minutes   Serves: 2

Preparation and Cooking Tips: you can also add some extra cream to the filling.

Serving Suggestion: Would you please serve the sandwich with an apple smoothie on the side?

Ingredients:

Rose orange blossom simple syrup:
- ⅛ teaspoon orange blossom water
- ½ cup granulated sugar
- 1 squeeze of lemon juice
- ⅛ teaspoon rose water
- ¼ cup water

Sandwiches:
- 4 slices bread, cut into 4 inches round

- 4 ounces mozzarella cheese, sliced
- Chopped pistachios, for garnish
- 4 teaspoons melted ghee
- 1 drop of orange food coloring
- 4 extra teaspoons of ghee
- ¾ cup kanafeh

Directions:

1. Mix all the sugar syrup ingredients in a saucepan and cook for 7 minutes on low heat with occasional stirring.
2. Mix melted ghee with orange food coloring in a bowl.
3. Preheat the Breakfast Sandwich Maker until the green PREHEAT light comes on.
4. Lift cover, top rings, and cooking plates. Place a bread slice inside the bottom tray of the sandwich maker.
5. Spread ½ of the knife, cheese, pistachios, and sugar syrup on top. Now lower the cooking plate and top rings.
6. Place another bread slice on top and brush it with a ghee mixture. Cover the top hood, and let the sandwich cook for 5 minutes.
7. Rotate the handle of the cooking plate clockwise until it stops.
8. Lift the hood, and the rings and transfer the sandwich to a plate.
9. Repeat the same steps with the remaining ingredients.

Nutritional Value (Amount per Serving):

Calories: 185; Fat: 8g; Sodium: 146mg; Carbs: 5g; Fiber: 0.1g; Sugar: 0.4g; Protein: 1g

Brie Strawberry Cheese Muffin Sandwich

Prep Time: 15 Minutes   Cook Time: 5 Minutes   Serves: 1

Preparation and Cooking Tips: Add some additional ground black pepper to the filling.

Serving Suggestion: Serve the sandwich with crispy bacon and your favorite sauce on the side.

Ingredients:

- 1-ounce brie, rind removed, and sliced
- 2 tablespoons sliced strawberries
- 1 English muffin, cut in half
- 1 ounce sliced smoked turkey

- 1 fresh basil leaves, sliced
- ½ tablespoon pepper jelly
- ½ tablespoon butter, melted

Directions:

1. Preheat the Breakfast Sandwich Maker until the green PREHEAT light comes on.
2. Lift cover, top rings, and cooking plates.
3. Place the lower half of the muffin in the sandwich maker and top it with butter and brie.
4. Now lower the cooking plate and top rings, then add turkey and the rest of the fillings.
5. Place another muffin half on top.
6. Cover the top hood, and let the sandwich cook for 5 minutes.
7. When finished cooking, rotate the handle of the cooking plate clockwise until it stops.
8. Lift the hood, and the rings and transfer the sandwich to a plate.

Nutritional Value (Amount per Serving):

Calories: 102; Fat: 7.6g; Sodium: 545mg; Carbs: 1.5g; Fiber: 0.4g; Sugar: 0.7g; Protein: 7.1g

Grilled Ham Toasties with Taleggio Cheese

Prep Time: 15 Minutes   Cook Time: 5 Minutes   Serves: 2

Preparation and Cooking Tips: Add some additional ground black pepper to the filling.

Serving Suggestion: Serve the sandwich with your favorite sauce on the side.

Ingredients:

- 4 slices of sandwich bread, cut into a 4-inch circle
- 4 tablespoons Taleggio cheese - rind removed
- 6 teaspoons butter soft
- 2 ham slices, grilled

Directions:

1. Preheat the Breakfast Sandwich Maker until the green PREHEAT light comes on.
2. Lift cover, top rings, and cooking plates.
3. Place one bread slice in the sandwich maker and top it with butter.
4. Lower the cooking plate and top rings then add ½ of the cheese and ham.
5. Add the other circle of the bread on top.
6. Cover the top hood, and let the sandwich cook for 5

minutes.

7. When finished cooking, rotate the handle of the cooking plate clockwise until it stops.
8. Lift the hood, and the rings and transfer the sandwich to a plate.
9. Repeat the same steps with the remaining ingredients.

Nutritional Value (Amount per Serving):

Calories: 305; Fat: 25g; Sodium: 532mg; Carbs: 2.3g; Fiber: 0.4g; Sugar: 2g; Protein: 18.3g

Dulce De Leche with Strawberries

Prep Time: 15 Minutes   Cook Time: 5 Minutes   Serves: 4

Preparation and Cooking Tips: You can also add a drizzle of paprika on top of the filling.

Serving Suggestion: Serve the sandwich with your favorite sauce on the side.

Ingredients:

- 8 large marshmallows, cut into 4 slices
- 4 tablespoons Dulce de Leche
- 4 large croissants, cut in half
- 8 strawberries, sliced   • Cooking spray

Directions:

1. Preheat the Breakfast Sandwich Maker until the green PREHEAT light comes on.
2. Lift cover, top rings, and cooking plates. Use the cooking spray.
3. Place the lower half of a croissant in the sandwich maker and top it with ¼ th of the Dulce de Leche.
4. Lower the cooking plate and top rings, then add ¼ th of the strawberries and marshmallows.
5. Place the other half of the croissant on top.
6. Cover the top hood, and let the sandwich cook for 5 minutes.
7. When finished cooking, rotate the handle of the cooking plate clockwise until it stops.
8. Lift the hood, and the rings and transfer the sandwich to a plate.
9. Repeat the same steps with the remaining ingredients.

Nutritional Value (Amount per Serving):

Calories: 284; Fat: 7.9g; Sodium: 704mg; Carbs: 38.1g; Fiber: 1.9g; Sugar: 1.9g; Protein: 14.8g

Honey Apple Pie

Prep Time: 15 Minutes   Cook Time: 5 Minutes   Serves: 4

Preparation and Cooking Tips: You can also add lettuce leaves to the filling.

Serving Suggestion: Serve the sandwich with your favorite sauce on the side.

Ingredients:

- 8 slices cinnamon raisin bread, cut into a 4-inch circle
- 1 Granny Smith apple, cored and sliced
- 2 Tablespoons light brown sugar
- ½ cup mascarpone cheese
- 2 teaspoons honey
- 4 tablespoons (½ stick) butter

Directions:

1. Blend mascarpone cheese with honey, sugar and butter.
2. Preheat the Breakfast Sandwich Maker until the green PREHEAT light comes on.
3. Lift cover, top rings, and cooking plates.
4. Place one bread slice in the sandwich maker and top it with ¼ cheese mixture.
5. Now lower the cooking plate and top rings then add ¼ apples on top.
6. Add the other circle of the bread on top. Cover the top hood, and let the sandwich cook for 5 minutes.
7. When finished cooking, rotate the handle of the cooking plate clockwise until it stops.
8. Lift the hood, and the rings and transfer the sandwich to a plate.
9. Repeat the same steps with the remaining ingredients.

Nutritional Value (Amount per Serving):

Calories: 183; Fat: 15g; Sodium: 402mg; Carbs: 2.5g; Fiber: 0.4g; Sugar: 1.1g; Protein: 10g

Turkey Cranberry Panini

Prep Time: 15 Minutes   Cook Time: 5 Minutes   Serves: 1

Preparation and Cooking Tips: You can also add lettuce leaves to the filling.

Serving Suggestion: Serve the sandwich with coleslaw and your favorite sauce on the side.

Ingredients:

- 2 slices of thick bread, cut into a 4-inch circle

- 1 tablespoon of cranberry sauce
- 1 tablespoon butter
- A few slices of turkey
- A few sage leaves
- 1-ounce goat cheese
- 2 slices cooked bacon
- 1 slice Muenster cheese

Directions:

1. Preheat the Breakfast Sandwich Maker until the green PREHEAT light comes on.
2. Lift cover, top rings, and cooking plates.
3. Place a bread slice in the sandwich maker and top it with sauce.
4. Now lower the cooking plate and top rings, then add the rest of the fillings.
5. Add the other circle of the bread on top.
6. Cover the top hood, and let the sandwich cook for 5 minutes.
7. When finished cooking, rotate the handle of the cooking plate clockwise until it stops.
8. Lift the hood, and the rings and transfer the sandwich to a plate.

Nutritional Value (Amount per Serving):

Calories: 180; Fat: 3.2g; Sodium: 133mg; Carbs: 32g; Fiber: 1.1g; Sugar: 1.8g; Protein: 9g

Cinnamon Blueberry Muffin Hand Pies

Prep Time: 15 Minutes   Cook Time: 12 Minutes   Serves: 6

Preparation and Cooking Tips: You can also add chocolate chips to the filling.

Serving Suggestion: Serve the pies with chocolate sauce on the side.

Ingredients:

- 6 English muffins, cut in half
- ½ teaspoon ground cinnamon
- 1 tablespoon fresh lemon juice
- 3 tablespoons cornstarch
- 1 teaspoon lemon zest
- 2½ cups fresh blueberries
- 2 tablespoons of water
- Sugar, for sprinkling
- ½ cup sugar
- A pinch of salt
- 1 egg yolk

Directions:

1. Mix blueberries with lemon juice, zest, cinnamon, salt, sugar, and cornstarch in a saucepan.
2. Stir and cook berries on low heat for 7 minutes. Allow this berry filling to cool at room temperature.
3. Preheat the Breakfast Sandwich Maker until the green PREHEAT light comes on.
4. Lift cover, top rings, and cooking plates. Place half of a muffin inside the bottom tray of the sandwich maker.
5. Add the egg yolk and a tablespoon of berry filling to its center. Place the other half of the muffin on top.
6. Now lower the cooking plate and top rings. Cover the top hood, and let the sandwich cook for 5 minutes.
7. Rotate the handle of the cooking plate clockwise until it stops.
8. Lift the hood, and the rings and transfer the sandwich to a plate.
9. Make more berry pies in the same way.

Nutritional Value (Amount per Serving):

Calories: 351; Fat: 19g; Sodium: 412mg; Carbs: 13g; Fiber: 0.3g; Sugar: 1g; Protein: 23g

Made in the USA
Middletown, DE
11 December 2024

66765712R00064